Scarecrow Studies in Young Adult Literature
Series Editor: Patty Campbell

Scarecrow Studies in Young Adult Literature is intended to continue the body of critical writing established in Twayne's Young Adult Authors Series and to expand it beyond single-author studies to explorations of genres, multicultural writing, and controversial issues in young adult (YA) reading. Many of the contributing authors of the series are among the leading scholars and critics of adolescent literature, and some are YA novelists themselves.

The series is shaped by its editor, Patty Campbell, who is a renowned authority in the field, with a thirty-year background as critic, lecturer, librarian, and teacher of YA literature. Patty Campbell was the 2001 winner of the ALAN Award, given by the Assembly on Adolescent Literature of the National Council of Teachers of English for distinguished contribution to YA literature. In 1989 she was the winner of the American Library Association's Grolier Award for distinguished service to young adults and reading.

1. *What's So Scary about R. L. Stine?* by Patrick Jones, 1998.
2. *Ann Rinaldi: Historian and Storyteller*, by Jeanne M. McGlinn, 2000.
3. *Norma Fox Mazer: A Writer's World*, by Arthea J. S. Reed, 2000.
4. *Exploding the Myths: The Truth about Teens and Reading*, by Marc Aronson, 2001.
5. *The Agony and the Eggplant: Daniel Pinkwater's Heroic Struggles in the Name of YA Literature*, by Walter Hogan, 2001.
6. *Caroline Cooney: Faith and Fiction*, by Pamela Sissi Carroll, 2001.
7. *Declarations of Independence: Empowered Girls in Young Adult Literature, 1990–2001*, by Joanne Brown and Nancy St. Clair, 2002.
8. *Lost Masterworks of Young Adult Literature*, by Connie S. Zitlow, 2002.
9. *Beyond the Pale: New Essays for a New Era*, by Marc Aronson, 2003.
10. *Orson Scott Card: Writer of the Terrible Choice*, by Edith S. Tyson, 2003.
11. *Jacqueline Woodson: "The Real Thing,"* by Lois Thomas Stover, 2003.

12. *Virginia Euwer Wolff: Capturing the Music of Young Voices*, by Suzanne Elizabeth Reid, 2003.
13. *More Than a Game: Sports Literature for Young Adults*, Chris Crowe, 2004.
14. *Humor in Young Adult Literature: A Time to Laugh*, by Walter Hogan, 2005.
15. *Life Is Tough: Guys, Growing Up, and Young Adult Literature*, by Rachelle Lasky Bilz, 2004.
16. *Sarah Dessen: From Burritos to Box Office*, by Wendy J. Glenn, 2005.
17. *American Indian Themes in Young Adult Literature*, by Paulette F. Molin, 2005.
18. *The Heart Has Its Reasons: Young Adult Literature with Gay/Lesbian/Queer Content, 1969–2004*, by Michael Cart and Christine A. Jenkins, 2006.
19. *Karen Hesse*, by Rosemary Oliphant-Ingham, 2005.
20. *Graham Salisbury: Island Boy*, by David Macinnis Gill, 2005.
21. *The Distant Mirror: Reflections on Young Adult Historical Fiction*, by Joanne Brown and Nancy St. Clair, 2006.
22. *Sharon Creech: The Words We Choose to Say*, by Mary Ann Tighe, 2006.
23. *Angela Johnson: Poetic Prose*, by KaaVonia Hinton, 2006.
24. *David Almond: Memory and Magic*, by Don Latham, 2006.
25. *Aidan Chambers: Master Literary Choreographer*, by Betty Greenway, 2006.
26. *Passions and Pleasures: Essays and Speeches about Literature and Libraries*, by Michael Cart, 2007.
27. *Names and Naming in Young Adult Literature*, by Alleen Pace Nilsen and Don L. F. Nilsen, 2007.

Names and Naming in Young Adult Literature

Alleen Pace Nilsen
Don L. F. Nilsen

Scarecrow Studies in
Young Adult Literature, No. 27

THE SCARECROW PRESS, INC.
Lanham, Maryland • Toronto • Plymouth, UK
2007

SCARECROW PRESS, INC.

Published in the United States of America
by Scarecrow Press, Inc.
A wholly owned subsidiary of
The Rowman & Littlefield Publishing Group, Inc.
4501 Forbes Boulevard, Suite 200, Lanham, Maryland 20706
www.scarecrowpress.com

Estover Road
Plymouth PL6 7PY
United Kingdom

British Library Cataloguing in Publication Information Available

Library of Congress Cataloging-in-Publication Data

Nilsen, Alleen Pace.
  Names and naming in young adult literature / Alleen Pace Nilsen, Don L. F.
Nilsen.
    p. cm. — (Scarecrow studies in young adult literature ; no. 27)
  Includes bibliographical references (p.   ) and index.
  ISBN-13: 978-0-8108-5808-4 (alk. paper)
  ISBN-10: 0-8108-5808-8 (alk. paper)
  1. Young adult literature, American—History and criticism. 2. Young adult
literature, English—History and criticism. 3. Names, Personal, in literature. 4.
Names in literature. 5. Characters and characteristics in literature. I. Nilsen,
Don Lee Fred. II. Title.

PS490.N57 2007
810.9'9283—dc22

                                                                    2007011281

♾™ The paper used in this publication meets the minimum requirements of
American National Standard for Information Sciences—Permanence of
Paper for Printed Library Materials, ANSI/NISO Z39.48-1992.
Manufactured in the United States of America.

To
Patty Campbell,
who, except for Beatrice (see chapter 7),
is the most dedicated person
we know in young adult literature

Contents

Introduction   Names and Naming in Young
Adult Literature   ix

Chapter 1   Names for Fun: M. E. Kerr, Gary Paulsen,
Louis Sachar, and Polly Horvath   1

Chapter 2   Names to Establish Tone and Mode:
Robert Cormier and Francesca Lia Block   23

Chapter 3   Names to Establish Time Periods:
Karen Cushman and Her Historical Fiction   47

Chapter 4   Names to Establish Realistic Settings:
Gary Soto, Adam Rapp, Meg Rosoff, and
Nancy Farmer   65

Chapter 5   Names to Establish Imagined Settings:
Yann Martel, Orson Scott Card, and
Ursula K. Le Guin   83

Chapter 6   Names to Reveal Ethnic Values: Amy Tan,
             Sandra Cisneros, Maya Angelou, Cynthia
             Kadohata, Sherman Alexie, and Others   103

Chapter 7   Names to Build a Dual Audience: Daniel
             Handler and the Lemony Snicket Books   123

Chapter 8   Names as Memory Hooks: J. K. Rowling
             and the Harry Potter Books   141

Bibliography   161

Index   167

About the Authors   173

~

Introduction: Names and Naming in Young Adult Literature

Teenagers are vitally involved in developing their own identities as they say good-bye to who they were as children and hello to who they will be as adults. Their names are an important part of their identities, which may be at the root of our observation that, both in real life and in literature, young people are more interested in manipulating and presenting their names than are adults.

A good example of the egocentricity of youth in relation to their own names is what an Associated Press reporter found when he went to Ernest Hemingway's old high school and looked through the 1916–1917 yearbook. He found that Hemingway had experimented with eight different pen names: Ernest Hemingway, Ernest Miller Hemingway, Ernest MacNamara Hemingway, Ernest Monhahan Hemingway, Ernest Hemingway. (with a period), Ernest Michealowitch Hemingway, B. S., and just E. H.[1] Not all teenagers are as motivated as was Hemingway to become a famous writer, but all teenagers give considerable thought to what they want to do with their lives, not just in relation to earning a living, but also to personal and spiritual aspects of their lives and how they want other people to relate to them.

Leslie Dunkling, in *The Guinness Book of Names*, observes that adults change their names in relation to marriage or a desire to separate different parts of their lives, but other than in these situations when adults change their names they usually do it under a cloud. They want to hide from someone or something or they want to make a new start in life. In contrast, when young adults change their names it is usually done in a celebratory mood filled with optimism and anticipation. A good illustration is near the beginning of F. Scott Fitzgerald's *The Great Gatsby*.

> James Gatz—that was really, or at least legally, his name. He had changed it at the age of seventeen and at the specific moment that witnessed the beginning of his career—when he saw Dan Cody's yacht drop anchor over the most insidious flat on Lake Superior. It was James Gatz who had been loafing along the beach that afternoon in a torn green jersey and a pair of canvas pants, but it was already Jay Gatsby who borrowed a rowboat, pulled out to the *Tuolumne* and informed Cody that a wind might catch him and break him up in half an hour.
>
> I suppose he'd had the name ready for a long time, even then. (98)

As you read chapters 1 through 8, we think you will be surprised at the variety of books we discuss and at the multitude of purposes for which the authors have incorporated names and processes of naming. However, we should caution that in our eagerness to demonstrate the different effects that skilled authors bring about through their manipulation of names, we have made some arbitrary decisions. Rather than being comprehensive, we present a sampling in hopes of inspiring readers to make their own observations. Authors capitalize on the freedom they have in creating names because with every other part of language they are controlled by what society has already agreed upon as the meanings of chosen sounds and how they should be represented. With names, authors can use all that they know about language to create totally new sound combinations and to clip and blend old names to be spelled and used in new ways. Names are the one part of language that gives all of us the control that Lewis Carroll's Humpty Dumpty claimed for himself: "When I use a word it means just what I choose it to mean—neither more nor less." As we've written this book, we have thought of six reasons that at least partly explain why young adults are especially responsive to authors who are skilled in the literary uses of names—not just personal names, but also place names and names for events, inventions, animals, attitudes, social developments, and imagined concepts.

1. *Teenagers are more interested than are adults in manipulating and presenting names.* Today's generation of young people have grown up with computers and with instant messaging and with their own passwords and e-mail addresses. We are sometimes appalled at how much information our college students reveal about themselves in the few letters it takes to make an e-mail address. Now that we are advised to change our passwords every 180 days and to include at least eight characters, more of us are getting practice in this kind of creativity, but we had no need to create new "identifications" for ourselves until the 1970s when the short-lived fad of CB radios demanded "handles." Some of us have taken advantage of the opportunity to create our own license plates, but as far as we know, the art of tagging, which is different from graffiti, is strictly a youth activity. According to Anne Winter, an ASU linguist who studied tagging in metropolitan Phoenix, taggers try to write their *tag* or nickname as often and as artistically as possible. Their motivation is simply to *get up*, to put one's name in front of the public and to acquire fame "through frequency and volume."[2]

2. *Today's media makes everyone more aware of people creating their own names.* When Toni Morrison won the Nobel Prize, newspapers wrote "Morrison was born Chloe Anthony Wofford in the steel-mill city of Lorain, Ohio." In other news stories, we have seen comedian Whoopi Goldberg's birth name given as Caryn Johnson, Engelbert Humperdinck's as Arnold Dorsey, and Danny Kaye's as David Daniel Kaminsky. The practice of adopting new and unusual names is especially common among musicians, who are some of teenagers' most admired heroes. Virtually everyone recognizes that such names as Bo Diddley, Fats Domino, Beenie Man, Bono, Ice-T, Snoop Dogg, and Eminem are not "birth names." Group names are even more creative, as with Guns N' Roses and the Sex Pistols with such aggressive performer names as Johnny Rotten and Sid Vicious. Athletes are another group whose nicknames teenagers admire, as with football players

Sweetness (Walter Payton), baseball players Charlie Hustle (Pete Rose) and Slammin' Sammy Sosa, and basketball players Magic Earvin Johnson and Sir Charles Barkley. Just as in real life where the best nicknames reflect an important aspect of personality, the most appreciated name changes in YA books are those that define the theme of the book, as do the titles of Christopher Paul Curtis's *Bud, Not Buddy*, Jerry Spinelli's *Maniac McGee*, and Joan Bauer's *Hope Was Here*.

3. *Teenagers are closer to the name games they played as children.* Linguists tell us that young brains are better equipped than adult brains to learn language, which is one of the reasons that seven- and eight-year-olds love riddles and knock-knock jokes. It is also one of the reasons they create nicknames for their classmates and give derogatory names to their teachers. When folklore collector Alvin Schwartz spoke at a humor conference on our campus, he made the point that children are basically powerless in their relationships with adults and so they seek emotional relief through name play. His observation stuck in our minds because we had just had an example in our family. One of our sons was in middle school and we overheard him talking with some friends about a teacher they called Harry. We knew he didn't have a teacher named Harry, and when we questioned him he cheerfully explained they called him Harry because his name was Dick. Adults are more likely to get this kind of emotional relief from sharing anecdotes about something stupid their boss did, from reading *Dilbert* cartoons, or from watching late-night-television comedians make fun of the rich and the powerful. Because young people know that making up hostile names for people is one of their techniques, Cynthia Voigt was especially effective in her negative portrayal of Tish's abusive stepfather, Tonnie, in *When She Hollers*. Tonnie tries to humiliate Tish by reversing the sounds of her name. Perceptive readers understand from this incident that he is not only cruel but also immature.

4. *People feel free to play with place names because they are not as sacred as they used to be.* People are taking a fresh look at the names of towns and public buildings because commercial interests have entered the picture and naming rights are being sold for everything

from colleges to sports events, and from state highways to whole towns. One of the first towns to change its name for free publicity was Hot Springs, New Mexico, which in 1950 took the name of Truth or Consequences to pay the popular radio quiz show for broadcasting from their town. More recent changes that have been in the news include the town of Agra, Oklahoma, which temporarily changed its name to Viagra to get free concert tickets, and the town of Halfway, Oregon, which became Half.Com for one year in exchange for money and computers. Bigger stakes are involved when naming rights are sold for athletic facilities, such as here in Arizona where Bank One Ballpark, commonly called BOB, was changed to Chase Field because JPMorgan Chase & Co. purchased Bank One. Phoenicians are grateful that Chase Field at least sounds semantically connected to a sport, unlike athletic facilities in some cities that are now called Gillette Stadium, AT&T Park, and ALLTEL Stadium. Authors of books for teens are joining in thinking of new ways to get mileage out of place names. Brian Meehl's *Out of Patience* is the humorous story of Jake Waters and his father's dream of opening the American Toilet Museum in their hometown of Patience, Kansas, while the titles of Kate Kliss's *Deliver Us from Normal* and *Far from Normal* were inspired by the town of Normal, Illinois, which like many streets and some U.S. towns, was given the name because it was home to a teachers college. Such schools used to be called Normal Schools. In 2002–2003, the name Paris became popular for girls because of Paris Hilton's TV show *The Simple Life*. Other place names currently being given to both girls and boys include Montana, Dakota (Cody), Camden, and Madison. Some readers were surprised to learn that John Green's *Looking for Alaska*, which won the 2006 Printz Award, was not a travel adventure but the story of Miles Halter's first year at boarding school where he comes under the spell of Alaska Young, a girl described as "clever, funny, screwed-up, and dead sexy."

5. *Young adult literature is contemporary and so can reflect current trends.* One of the main reasons that teenagers enjoy reading YA literature, as opposed to the "classics" that are likely to be assigned in English classes, is that most of the authors are alive,

and because they are astute observers of today's society they use names in the "edgy" ways that students see in everyday life. Because today's fashion favors creative naming, some names that only a few years ago were considered "weird" have risen in popularity. When the Social Security Administration released its 2005 list of the top one hundred names for boys and for girls, people were surprised to see that Nevaeh (Heaven spelled backwards) had worked its way into the top one hundred for girls. Also rising in popularity were such spiritual names as Destiny, Trinity, and Miracle. According to an article in USA Today[3] in 1880 more than 50 percent of U.S. male infants were given one of the top twenty boys' names. Today the top twenty boys' names are given to only 20 percent of male infants. Girls have always had more variety in their names, but still in 1880, 34 percent of female infants were given one of the top twenty names. Today only 14 percent of girls will be given such common names. On websites dedicated to naming babies, parents are usually cautioned against choosing names for their children that will make a joke when first and last names are said together, but that doesn't keep authors from having such fun, as does Meg Rosoff in the first few pages of *Just in Case*, when her protagonist, David Case, changes his name to Justin. Donna Jo Napoli clipped the name of Rapunzel to get the title *Zel* for her retelling of the old story. This is similar to the way that Gail Carson Levine clipped Cinderella's name for the title of her *Ella Enchanted*.

6. *People are choosing names to honor, or at least hint at, ethnic identifications.* Boxer Cassius Clay was one of the first celebrities to do this when he changed his name to Mohammad Ali. When the television journalist now known as Geraldo Rivera graduated from law school and began practicing in New York City, he used the Anglo-sounding name of Jerry Rivers, but when he went into show business he decided that a Latino identification would help him more. Akebono, the first American to win the Japanese sumo wrestling championship was born Chad Rowan in Oahu, Hawaii, but he changed it to a Japanese-sounding name to fit with the sport. More typically, many of today's parents are giving

their children ethnic-sounding names as a reflection of pride in their heritage. Of course when an author writes a book focused on exploring ethnic differences, there is much more involved than simply giving the characters ethnic-sounding names. Nevertheless, it is the titles of such books as *When My Name Was Keoko* by Linda Sue Park, *Call Me Maria* by Judith Ortiz Cofer, and *Missing Angel Juan* by Francesca Lia Block that serve to let readers know that the books are going to have something to say about particular ethnicities.

In this book, we define young adult literature as whatever readers between the ages of twelve and eighteen choose to read for their own pleasure or enlightenment. Such reading might be related either to school assignments or to leisure-time reading. Also, we do not restrict our definition to books published by youth divisions of publishing houses; for example, we are including books published for general adult audiences by Sherman Alexie, Maya Angelou, Orson Scott Card, Sandra Cisneros, Yann Martel, and Amy Tan, but "found" by young adults, who relate to them at least partly because of the young protagonists, but also, we think, because of how observant and clever these authors are in their uses of naming as a literary technique.

We hope to encourage teachers and librarians to add names and naming to their book discussions with young readers, but we shudder at the thought of fill-in-the-blank tests where students lose points for forgetting the names of minor characters or misspelling the names of major characters. We hope to inspire readers to make deeper connections and thereby gain added pleasure from reading many of the well-written books being produced for today's young adults.

In closing, we want to thank the late Robert Cormier, who when we interviewed him in 1979, gave us so many insights into what skilled authors can do with names, that we began reading with increased pleasure and a new interest in names. Without his generosity, we probably would not have thought of writing this book. We also want to express thanks to Arizona State University students Lisa Arter, Sandra Crandall, Elizabeth Dern, Morgan Langhofer, and Barbara Yost, who made numerous contributions both through their knowledge and enthusiasm, and to the English Education administrative assistants, Bonnie Rig-maiden and Erika L. Witt, for secretarial support.

Notes

1. Associated Press filler, reprinted in *Arizona Republic* (May 6, 1994).
2. Ann Winter, "Graffiti as Social Discourse" in *Living Language* edited by Alleen Pace Nilsen. Boston: Allyn & Bacon, 1999, 106–11.
3. Breanne Gilpatrick and Maria Puente, "Parents resort to old trick, pick 'vintage' baby names." *USA Today*, reprinted in *The Arizona Republic*, October 1, 2005.

~

CHAPTER ONE

Names for Fun: M. E. Kerr, Gary Paulsen, Louis Sachar, and Polly Horvath

While humor scholars cannot agree on exactly what will amuse people, they do agree that for something to be funny there have to be elements of surprise or incongruity. Not all surprises are funny, but everything that is funny contains something that is surprising. The pleasure comes to people when their minds make a connection between two (or more) unexpected or incongruous ideas.

To introduce this chapter and to illustrate some of the current theories about what—in addition to surprise—brings the intellectual pleasure of humor, we will outline some of the name-related features and functions of humor as described by literary critics and scholars. Our illustrations come from the books of M. E. Kerr, who since 1972, when she won accolades with *Dinky Hocker Shoots Smack*, has relied on names and naming practices to bring smiles, and sometimes outright giggles, to her readers. The features and functions listed here are representative rather than comprehensive because authors are always finding new ways to surprise and amuse people with names, as shown by the fuller examples presented in this chapter from books by Gary Paulsen, Louis Sachar, and Polly Horvath.

Names Expressing Hostility and/or Superiority

Some humor scholars believe that for any joke or incident to be funny it must contain the tension that goes along with the feelings of hostility or superiority that are reflected in such humor-related terms as *punch line, biting satire, sharp-tongued wit,* a *pointed remark,* a *barbed joke, to crack* (or *break*) *someone up, to knock 'em dead,* and *to bomb.* In *Night Kites,* when Nicki introduces her new boyfriend, Erick Rudd, to her dad, he grins and says, "A new one, Fickle Pickle? Well, what's your name? . . . Rudd?" Then he laughingly advises, "Don't let her make your name Mud, Rudd" (151).

In three different books (*Gentlehands, Love Is a Missing Person,* and *Night Kites*) Kerr makes jokes about the snobbishness of country clubs when she changes the name of the Hadefield Country Club to the Hate-Filled Club. In *Gentlehands,* she illustrates the tension that exists between ordinary townspeople and wealthy owners of seaside estates by having Buddy's father refer to Skye Pennington, the girl he has a crush on, as Miss Gottbucks from Beaublahblah. The Penningtons live on a five-acre estate named Beauregard and Buddy observes that

> They always seem to have names like that, don't they? Rich, beautiful girls are never named Elsie Pip or Mary Smith. They have these special names and they say them in their particular tones and accents, and my mother was right. I was in over my head or out of my depth, or however she put it. (1)

In *If I Love You, Am I Trapped Forever?* the protagonist is an ordinary high school boy named Alan, who leads the attack on a new student by calling him Doomed instead of his real name, Duncan. But the more the girls in school get to know this intellectual boy, who is so different from typical high school jocks, the more they like him. Alan is amazed when he hears his girlfriend refer to Doomed as Duncan. He expresses surprise and she says, "Alan, you couldn't believe I *care* anything about Dunc!" As Alan observes, "From Doomed to Duncan to Dunc was a long distance in a very short space of time" (135–36).

In her autobiographical *ME ME ME ME ME,* Kerr says that the boy who inspired the character of Duncan was a Jewish refugee named Hyman Ginzburg. He got off to a bad start in Auburn, New York, because the word *hyman* "was never spoken unless you were talking privately about the wedding night." He was called "Hyman the Hopeless" or just plain "Hopeless" (14).

Early in *Little Little*, which is a story about dwarves, Kerr uses names to establish a flip tone and to reveal the attitudes of the residents of the Twin Oaks Orphan's Home where Sidney Applebaum, a dwarf with a humpback, grows up. He lives in Miss Lake's—commonly called Mistake's—cottage. Other residents include legless Wheels Potter, who gets around on a custom-made skateboard; Bighead Langhorn, who has a short, skinny body but a head the size of an enormous pumpkin; Cloud, a one-armed albino with a "massive head of curly white hair"; and Pill Suchanek, whose mother took a drug during her pregnancy that left Pill with flippers for arms. The teacher is named Robert but the kids call him Robot because "his only facial expression was a smile, his only mood cheerful" (18–19). Miss Lake disapproves of this kind of dark humor and implores the boys not to call Albert Cloud because "His name is Albert Werman." Cloud insists that he likes the name because before he came to Twin Oaks he was "Albert Worm, or just plain Wormy" (63). What Miss Lake does not understand is that the boys have grabbed "naming rights" for themselves so as to take away the pain that might come from outsiders calling them names. In keeping with their attitude, they refer to "regular" people as Sara Lee, an acronym for Similar And Regular And Like Everyone Else.

Names Based on Wordplay

The above examples are "softened" by wordplay, which some humor scholars say is in itself a kind of hostility because the creators are showing that they are superior to the language because they can do things with sounds that other people have not thought of. Others say the pleasure or amusement, at least for the reader or listener—if not for the creator—comes simply from the surprise, as with the biggest midyear social event in *Him She Loves?* It is the Dead of Winter Dance and even though people are to come dressed as someone dead, the music will be "Live from Ironing Bored" (84).

Kerr loves using repetition and alliteration in creating such names as Little Little, Belle La Belle, Carolyn Cardmaker, Dirtie Dotti, Buddy

Boyle, and Gloria Gilman (nicknamed Gee Gee). She hints at the values of $uzy $lade by writing her name with dollar signs while she uses sarcasm in the name of Miss Grand from Videoland. Wally Witherspoon in *If I Love You, Am I Trapped Forever?* has an alliterative name that encourages Wally's "friends" to tease him about his family's mortuary business. They call him Wither Up and Die, Withering Heights, and Wither-Away. In *I Stay Near You*, the parents of rock star Saint Vincent named him after their favorite poet, Edna St. Vincent Millay, while the parents of Opal Ringer apparently named her after an opal ring.

In *ME ME ME ME ME*, Kerr quotes from her father's journal, "Our daughter is dating the local undertaker's son, Donald Dare, tall, dark, and harmless. Dares very little is my guess" (9). This sounds almost too "polished" to have really been written in a daily journal, but it is fun to read not just because of the alliteration and the pun, but also because the name scans the same as Donald Duck.

Kerr surprises and amuses her readers by creating character names which at first go unnoticed, but can later be used in a pun. For example in *Little Little*, Sydney Cinnamon is a catchy, alliterative name for the dwarf hero. Midway through the book when Andrea Applebaum's mother hires Sydney to be the baby at a New Year's Eve party, he and Andrea grow romantic in the basement and Andrea croons, "Cinnamon and Applebaum. Put us together and we're a pie" (101).

Kerr undoubtedly named John Fell, the hero of her three mystery novels, *Fell*, *Fell Back*, and *Fell Down*, with an eye to such additional puns as *fell apart*, *fell to pieces*, and *fell in love*. When he gets hired, or more accurately bribed, to attend the Gardner School in place of a boy named Thompson Pingree, but called Ping, readers get the image of how the boy that Fell is protecting is batted back and forth by his quarreling parents.

Names Based on Allusions

Unexpected allusions often bring incongruous images as when in *ME ME ME ME ME*, Kerr names the dormitories at her old school Little Dorrit, David Copperfield, Hard Times, and Great Expectations. This was partly to honor Charles Dickens, whose skill with names she has long admired, but also to provide fodder for clever punning. In *Dinky Hocker Shoots Smack*, the cat, which was found under a car, is named Nader in honor of Ralph Nader, who as a critic of the American automobile industry has also spent considerable time under cars.

In *ME ME ME ME ME*, the second story is entitled "Where Are You Now, William Shakespeare?" It is about Marijane's childhood "romance" with a ten-year-old neighbor named William Shakespeare, but called Billy for short. They both agree that if they ever marry and have a son they will name him Ellis (after her father) rather than William. Billy insists that this is not because William Shakespeare is a funny name; "It's just that there's a famous writer with the same name" (36).

In *Night Kites*, Erick has a crush on Nicki, whose father, Captain Marr (as in such sea-related words as *marine, maritime, marina,* and *marinara sauce*) runs the Kingdom by the Sea motel, which is a "tacky, shabby, shitty, going to rack and ruin" place, while at the same time bearing witness to having once "been a crazy, fantastic place: mysterious and silly and rare" (140–41). The suites that face the sea have Edgar Allan Poe names: Bells, Bells, Bells; The Raven; Helen; and The Black Cat. On some afternoons Nicki works at Anabel's Resale Shop, but on other afternoons, she and Erick swim at City by the Sea or make love in Dream within a Dream.

An example of a more generalized kind of allusion occurs in *I'll Love You When You're More Like Me*. The teenage television star Sabra St. Amour tells how her mother used to burst into her room, turn off Elvis, and say, "What are we doing lollygagging around here like Mrs. Average and her daughter, Mediocre? Let's go to the Apple for some fun!" (115). Sabra goes on to explain that this was way back in the "Dark Ages when Sam, Sam Superman" had them trapped in suburbia and Sabra's name was Maggie. Their glamorous new life is as different from the old as is Sabra's new name from her original name of Maggie Duggy.

Ironic Names

When authors say one thing while really meaning something else they are using irony, which forces readers to become intellectually involved in figuring out the deeper, as opposed to the surface, meaning. This is not a kind of humor that will make people laugh out loud, but they may smile inwardly when they realize that the protagonist of *Dinky Hocker Shoots Smack* is anything but "dinky." A more somber example is the title of Kerr's *Gentlehands*, which is based on the postwar hunt for one of the cruelest of the Nazi SS guards at Auschwitz, who taunted his Jewish prisoners from Rome by playing Puccini's opera *Tosca* and singing "O dolci mani," which translates as "gentle hands." The plot of the story centers around whether Buddy's mysterious German grandfather is this man. He has named his keeshond dog Mignon, a name that he says comes from an opera, but a more gruesome interpretation could be that it comes from *filet mignon*, as a reminder of how Gentlehands used to turn selected prisoners over to his dogs.

Another solemn example of irony occurs in the book *Linger*, which is about the 1992 Gulf War. In it, the soldier who was so beautiful that he was called Movie Star comes home from the war with his face practically blown away by "friendly fire," meaning that he was accidentally shot by soldiers on his own team. The term is so ironic that the military no longer uses it for such accidental injuries.

Names to Reveal Social Class and Attitudes

Is That You, Miss Blue? is set in a southern boarding school for young women. While most of the girls come from old, well-established families, a couple of them come from families that are newly affluent due to the discovery of oil on their land. Rather than going into a long, sociological description of the many differences this entails, Kerr puts across the idea by stating that Carolyn Cardmaker's roommate is named Cute Diblee, "and Cute isn't a nickname either. She's got a sister called Sweet" (33).

In the same book, one of the teachers, Ernestine Blue, is unusually religious. When Miss Blue puts a crucifixion painting in the bathroom, the girls ridicule her by devising such nicknames as O Torn Cheeks, Thorn-Brain, and O Fingers-Nailed. Flanders Brown, the protagonist of the story, is amazed when one of the other teachers tells her that she had gone to school with Ernestine Blue, who had been called Nesty and was chased by all the boys. Miss Blue teaches chemistry and reveals something about her own attitudes when she teaches the girls about snob gases, those "that refuse to combine with anything else under any conditions." She explains to the class that even though Cavendish, the discoverer of such gases as argon and neon, called them "noble gases because of their elite quality, she preferred to think of them as the snobs" (121).

In *Little Little*, Larry La Belle leaves little doubt about what he thinks of Little Little's two boyfriends. He calls the one who has a hunchback and makes extra money as the mascot for a pest control company the Roach. He refers to the other one, who is already known as Opportunity Knox because of the way he uses his dwarfism to attract followers to his fledging church, Mr. Clean or Mr. White Suit.

In *Gentlehands*, Buddy is surprised that one of Skye's wealthy friends who is named Conrad goes by Connie. In Buddy's crowd no self-respecting boy would have allowed himself to be called Connie. Later in the book, Skye tells Buddy that Connie Spreckles has a new Connie. When Buddy looks puzzled, she explains that he has a new Lincoln Continental, which everybody calls Connies. This patronizing scene appears near the end of the book and communicates to readers that Skye and Buddy are close to the end of their summer romance.

Humorous Names to Balance Serious Issues

Kerr's 1986 *Night Kites* is one of the earliest books to be written about a family's experience with AIDS. When their oldest son, Pete, comes home to die from the disease, Kerr counterbalances the basic sadness of the situation with names that make readers smile. For as long as Erick, the younger brother who tells the story, can remember, there has been tension between Pete and the boys' father. Pete used to call him O Infallible, but the younger Erick, who did not know the word *infallible*, sensed only the hostility and interpreted the name as "O Full of Bull."

Another bit of family history relating to Pete is that at age thirteen he knew he was gay and named his dog Oscar as a secret memorial to Oscar Wilde. The family's minister, Reverend Shorr, tries to be helpful during this difficult period, but the Rudd family still refers to him as Reverend Snore because he always reads his sermons, which sound like "instructions for assembling mail-order items" (126).

Among Kerr's best-known books is her 1994 *Deliver Us from Evie*, a story told by Parr Burrman, the younger brother of Evie, who is a gay senior in the small farming community of Duffton. The title comes from a hostile use of Evie's name when at church the Lord's Prayer is being recited and a boy says "in this loud voice, 'Deliver us from Evie,'" after which he nudges Evie and laughs as if he has made a good joke (91). The boy is named Cord Whittle, an appropriate name for a boy who wants to tie Evie down to the farm and perhaps at the same time whittle Patsy Duff down to size. Patsy is Evie's best friend as well as the daughter of the richest family in Duffton. A gold sign in front of their farm reads "Duffarm," while everyone knows that the Duffs paid for the Duffton Municipal Swimming Pool as well as the Duffton Community Center and the Veterans Memorial Statue. Playful names that lighten the tension of the story include that of Angel Kidder, who is a religious but fickle girl whom Parr has a crush on. The town sheriff has the last name of Starr, while his freckle-faced son is called Spots. When Evie's brother brings a girlfriend named Bella Hanna home from college, she turns out to be a vegetarian who turns up her nose at most of the things about their farm. Evie and Parr get even by referring to her as Anna Banana.

The Humor of Commercial Names

Teenagers are so often the targets of commercial advertising whether in their magazines, on television, or through "cookies" and "pop-up ads" on computer screens, that in their own defense they develop a veneer of cynicism about commercial messages. This means that they are especially appreciative of authors who make fun of advertisers' techniques. A common trick is to create product names that drop hints instead of making the kind of forthright claims that could be argued against. Kerr points this out when Wally first meets Sabra St. Amour on the beach in an early scene from *I'll Love You When You're More Like Me*. She asks him for a cigarette, and he tells her that she would have to be a little crazy to let the tobacco companies manipulate her with such names as Merit, which is supposed to mean something like excellence, or value, or a reward. He can't see anything excellent, valuable, or rewarding about having cancer. Sabra tells him she came to the beach for a swim and some sun, not for a lecture, but he goes on to ask her about the appropriateness of Vantage (clipped from advantage) as a brand name and whether True, More, and Now mean that you will get more out of life by living for the moment because you won't live long if you are being True to your filthy habit. Sabra doesn't quit smoking, but she does start to get interested in Wally as a thinker. In another acknowledgment of the power of commercial names, in *What I Really Think of You*, Opal's overweight mother is constantly eating Good & Plenty licorice candy while insisting that she doesn't "care one way or the other"; she just likes the name (170).

In *Fell* when John is working at the Plain and Fancy gourmet shop, one morning he forgets to put the raisins in their famous White Raisin Dream Cakes. Quick thinker that he is, he capitalizes on his forgetfulness by frosting and renaming them "Remembering Helen" in honor of his girlfriend, Keats, whose real name is Helen J. Keating. "What the hell does that mean?" barks the owner. Fell patiently explains that people like kinky names and the cakes are selling well. Then he suggests that they rename the Black Walnut Cake "Smiles We Left Behind Us." His unimpressed boss responds with "We're not in showbiz here" (55–56).

Another mysterious name in the *Fell* books is the secret Sevens Club at the elite Gardner school. The name hints at the students' good luck in being tapped for membership and the accompanying special privileges. Only near the end of the third book do readers learn that membership is awarded to those students who, at the freshman tree-planting ceremony, happen to choose a seven-letter name for their tree. As examples, Kerr lists Madonna, Cormier, and Up Yours. John had named his tree Good-bye partly because he had criticized his girlfriend's architect father for choosing the pretentious name of Adieu for the last house he planned to build. Another reason for his choice is that in coming to Gardner disguised as Thompson Pingree, he is saying goodbye to his old name, his old life, and his old friends.

In *Linger*, the Dunlinger family is accustomed to "owning" the restaurant business in their town. When a new little Mexican restaurant that brings out pitchers of sangria and lets people sit in a pretty little garden with twinkling lights threatens to compete, Bobby Dunlinger starts the rumor that the owners catch cats in the fields behind the canal and serve them up as part of their well-spiced Mexican food. The restaurant's name is Mañana, but to make sure everyone gets the point, Bobby uses graffiti to change the name to Mañana Meow.

Gary Paulsen's *How Angel Peterson Got His Name*

Gary Paulsen's *How Angel Peterson Got His Name* is a collection of five autobiographical stories—really six, counting the one in the foreword—about the wacky things that Paulsen and his buddies experience while growing up in rural Minnesota. He dedicates the book to "all boys in their thirteenth year; the miracle is that we live through it."

Three of the stories, including the one that gives the book its title, revolve around names:

> Carl Peterson—that's the name his mother and father gave him, but from the age of thirteen and for the rest of his life not a soul, not his wife or children or any friend has ever known him by that name.
>
> He is always called Angel.
>
> Angel Peterson, and I was there when he got his name. (1)

The story is too carefully written to spoil by retelling its thirty-four pages in just a few excerpts, so we will only say that the naming of Angel Peterson is where the story begins and where it ends. Paulsen uses the incident as the frame on which to hang some very funny writing.

In the second story, "The Miracle of Flight," Paulsen includes as almost a sidebar an incident telling how Willy Parnell got the nickname of Stinky Parnell while also breaking his right ankle and getting out of gym class "for the rest of the year" (41). Willy had bought a silk parachute at the Army Surplus Store. The biggest one he could afford was a freight parachute designed to carry eighty pounds of freight, "while Willy came in at a hundred and sixteen" (41). Nevertheless when he climbed to the top of the water tower and "unintentionally invented base jumping," he thought it was working except that "the ground seemed to be coming up pretty fast" and then he went through the roof of the Carlsons' chicken coop (40). "Several of the chickens and a goodly pile of chicken manure combined to break Willy's fall and keep him from killing himself" (41). Mrs. Carlson is quoted in the local newspaper under the headline "Boy Crashes Coop!" Her biggest worry is that the chickens will never lay again because "they have a powerful fear of hawks and they thought it was a giant hawk that came after them" (41). Stinky's new name comes from the way the chicken manure ground into his skin so that it takes more than a simple shower to get rid of it.

The third story "Orvis Orvisen and the Crash and Bash" begins with

> There are boys' names that you know will make a boy popular and suc-
> cessful and cool and able to talk to girls (more on this later) and will
> make him have a wonderful life and probably get rich and marry a cheer-
> leader and have a hot car. . . .
>   Clint is such a name, and perhaps Steve, although not necessarily
> Steven, and Brad, and maybe best of all Nick. You just know that some-
> body named Nick is going to get it all.
>   And then there are the other names. (55)

Paulsen mentions such names as Harvey and Sidney and Gary and
Wesley and empathizes with any poor boy so naïve as to stand "up in the
back of a new class and say, 'Hello, my name is Harvey Hemesvedt'—not
Harv, or Sid or Wes, but the whole name, Harvey" (56). All this is by way
of introducing the title character in the story whose parents were "silly or
addled or just plain cruel enough to give him the first name of Orvis so
he has to say, 'Hello, my name is Orvis Orvisen.'" Paulsen says they might
as well have just rubbed "him with raw liver" and thrown "him into a pit
of starving wolves" (56). Everything that happens to Orvis in the story—
and there is plenty that happens—Paulsen chalks up to the way that
Orvis's personality has been molded by having been given the heavy bur-
den of carrying around such a name as Orvis Orvisen.

In the last story, "And Finally, Skateboards, Bungee Jumping and
Other Failures" Paulsen adds a different kind of naming humor when
Wayne, riding a two-by-four with skate wheels nailed to the side, grabs
onto the bumper of a car whose unsuspecting driver is on his way to
Hutchinson, seven miles away. The boys tire of waiting for Wayne to
come back and so they hitch their way back into town and go to the
drugstore for "Coke glasses filled with ice cream covered with chocolate sauce and peanuts which were called, I swear, Little Dicks." The
boys could never look at the sign

LITTLE DICKS
15 CENTS

without breaking into a knowing smile (100).

Louis Sachar's *Holes* and *Small Steps*

Seldom has an author had so much fun with names as did Louis Sachar in *Holes*, which in 1999 won the Newbery Medal and in 1998 the National Book Award. The story is basically a tragedy, but Sachar's name play keeps it from being grim. It is actually two stories, one historical and one contemporary. The protagonist is Stanley Yelnats, whose surname is a backwards spelling of his given name. The name can be traced back to the "old country" where Elya Yelnats (later to be known as the infamous "no-good-dirty-rotten-pig-stealing-great-great-grandfather") falls in love with the beautiful but "pot-headed" Myra.

A middle-aged pig farmer named Igor Barkov has already offered Myra's father a pig weighing fifty stones, but the father says he has to wait until Myra turns fifteen. Elya is heartbroken because he has nothing to offer. Madame Zeroni, a kindhearted fortune-teller, advises Elya that he will be better off to go to America as her son has already done, but when she sees how sad he is she gives him a runt pig "not much bigger than a rat" and advises him to carry it to the top of a nearby mountain, and when at the top to sing it a song that she teaches him and to let the pig drink from the fresh springwater (30). She promises Elya that each day he will grow stronger just as the pig grows bigger, and that by the time Myra turns fifteen, he will have a competitive pig. Then she asks for just one more thing:

> "Anything," said Elya.
> "I want you to carry me up the mountain. I want to drink from the stream, and I want you to sing the song to me."
> Elya promised he would.
> Madame Zeroni warned that if he failed to do this, he and his descendants would be doomed for all of eternity. (31)

When on her fifteenth birthday, the empty-headed Myra cannot make up her mind about whether to marry Elya or Igor (she tells them each to choose a number between one and ten), Elya is so disgusted that he gives her the pig for a wedding present and goes directly to the dock where he boards a ship to America. He forgets all about promising Madame Zeroni that in appreciation for her giving him the runt piglet plus all of the advice, he will carry her up the mountain to drink from the spring. This is the beginning of the family curse that plagues the Yelnats family, through Elya's son, who takes the more "American" sounding first name of Stanley, and on through his son and his son, ending up with the Stanley Yelnats who is the protagonist of *Holes*. Readers meet the youngest Stanley Yelnats as he is being checked into Camp Green Lake, a juvenile detention center in the middle of a Texas desert.

The story is filled with ironies, starting with the name of Camp Green Lake. The lake has been dry so long that it is now part of a barren desert and has the shape of a frying pan. It is filled with holes because every day each boy in the camp must dig a hole as deep and as wide as his shovel. The boys are told they are digging the holes to build character, but they suspect something more because they are instructed to bring anything unusual that they find to their leaders.

One of the ways the boys take out their resentment is by refusing to address the leaders by their real names. The less awful of the two male counselors (or guards) is Mr. Pendanski, who explains that all the boys need to remember his name is *Pen*, *Dance*, and *Key*. Instead, they call him Mom. They are only borderline disrespectful to the other guard who wants to be addressed as Sir. In feigned innocence they call him Mr. Sir.

They seldom interact with Warden Walker and are so terrified of her that they would not think of giving her a nickname. However, Sachar uses her family name to tie her to Trout Walker, the bully of the original town of Green Lake, who in the late 1800s burns Kate Barlow's school and kills her African American boyfriend, Onion Sam, as well as his donkey, Mary Lou. He also sinks Onion Sam's boat, which was named after Mary Lou, the donkey. The sheriff refuses to help because Kate Barlow will not kiss him, and so, three days after the mayhem, Kate Barlow walks into the sheriff's office and shoots him dead. Then, she applies a fresh coat of red lipstick and gives him the kiss he was asking for. Since that fateful day, not a drop of water has fallen on Camp Green Lake.

This event is the beginning of her twenty-year rampage as Kissin' Kate, who robs stagecoaches as they cross the Texas desert. When she retires and comes back to live at Green Lake, she has been there only three months when she is awakened by someone breaking into her cabin. She opens her eyes and sees a blurry rifle only two inches from her nose. She smells Trout Walker's dirty feet and sees a redheaded woman rummaging through her cupboards and drawers and knocking things from Kate's shelves. The woman comes to her demanding:

> "Where is it?" . . .
> "Linda Miller?" asked Kate. "Is that you?"
> Linda Miller had been in the fourth grade when Kate Barlow was still a teacher. She had been a cute freckle-faced girl with beautiful red hair. Now her face was blotchy, and her hair was dirty and scraggly.
> "It's Linda Walker now," said Trout.
> "Oh, Linda, I'm so sorry," said Kate.
> Trout jabbed her throat with the rifle. "Where's the loot?" (121)

Kissin' Kate does not tell Trout and Linda where the treasure is, and when they force her on a walk through the desert she is bitten by one of the deadly poisonous yellow-spotted lizards and dies laughing because she has kept her secret. Warden Walker is the child of Trout and Linda, and remembers that as a child even on Christmas she was digging holes in search of the missing treasure. She founded Camp Green Lake Detention Center mainly to get strong young boys like Stanley to do the digging.

The boys in the tent to which Stanley is assigned have a variety of nicknames designed to fit their individual personalities. Armpit "earns" his nickname by making the mistake of complaining when the infection and the pain from a scorpion bite gathers in the lymph nodes under his arm. Hector Zeroni is called Zero not just as a shortened form of his name, but as an insulting description of what the boys think is in his head because he is unusually quiet and does not know how to read. The "gang leader" apparently creates his own name of X-Ray as compensation for the fact that he has bad eyes. His explanation is that it is pig Latin for his real name of Rex. Zigzag walks funny, Magnet steals things, Squid is small, and Barf Bag, the boy whose smelly cot Stanley inherits, apparently threw up on a regular basis. When the book opens, Barf Bag is out of the picture because of having been taken to a hospital after being bitten by a rattlesnake. His real name is Lewis and the callousness of the camp is shown by the fact that no one asks about him. He may have even died. Something similar happens later in the book when Zero runs away and his bed is immediately given to a new-comer. The boy is called Twitch because whenever he walks by a good-looking car his fingers start twitching at the challenge of seeing if he can steal it. When Stanley hears someone call out to "Caveman," he looks around to see who else has come into the tent, and then in sur-prise realizes that this is his new name. Back at school where he was picked on by the bully Derrick Dunne, whose given name is the same as the surname of the famous English executioner who devised *derricks* from which to hang people, Stanley had felt large and awkward, so now he kind of likes the "macho" sound of his new name.

The two most important names in the story are those of Stanley Yel-nats and Hector Zeroni. In the end, readers discover that Zero is a de-scendant of the original Madame Zeroni. He is the closest to a friend that Stanley has at Camp Green Lake. Stanley had been teaching Zero to read and Zero had been helping Stanley dig his holes. When Zero gets so tired of being picked on that he runs away, Stanley decides to go after him. He finds Zero hiding in the remains of a wrecked boat, very sick from eating and drinking the only thing that was available: brandied peaches (called Sploosh) prepared 110 years ago by Kissin' Kate and given to Onion Sam as a love gift. Stanley helps the very weak Zero to come with him in search of the Thumb of God, an un-usual geographical outcropping that Stanley's great-great-grandfather talked about as having saved his life because of being home to a natu-ral spring, even though it is on top of a mountain across the desert from what is now Camp Green Lake. Stanley and Zero have a challenging journey, but they succeed in making it to the Thumb of God, where they find both water to drink and onions to eat. Once their strength is restored they secretly climb back to Camp Green Lake to dig one more hole near where Stanley had found a lipstick tube engraved with the initials K. B. And sure enough in the middle of the night, they find a suitcase with a name on the outside, which Zero recognizes as Stanley, spelled backwards. It is the long lost treasure hidden by Kissin' Kate af-ter she stole it from Stanley's Great-Great-Grandfather Yelnats.

When daylight comes, the warden, Mr. Pendanski, and Mr. Sir gather around the hole but are afraid to touch Stanley and Zero because of the dreaded yellow-spotted lizards. The lizards don't bite Stanley or Zero because they are repelled by the smell and the taste of onions, and so the story ends happily. Stanley's father has hired a lawyer to help protect his invention of foot deodorant, and on the side, the lawyer begins investigating Stanley's assignment to Camp Green Lake. She comes to get Stanley released but has to leave because no one knows where he is. The next day she returns with the state attorney general, and in the end, Stanley and Zero each receive something less than—but not a lot less than—a million dollars.

In one of the greatest ironies, Camp Green Lake is "bought by a national organization dedicated to the well-being of young girls. In a few years, Camp Green Lake will become a Girl Scout Camp" (227). What makes this so ironic is that all through the book Mr. Sir has been sarcastically calling the boys Girl Scouts and saying things like "You're not in the Girl Scouts anymore," and asking them, "You Girl Scouts having a good time?" At the very end when the official-looking car arrives bringing the attorney general and Stanley's lawyer, he rightly observes that "It ain't Girl Scouts selling cookies" (211).

Another ironic name is that of Sweet Feet Livingston, a baseball player who specializes in stealing bases. While Livingston's "sweet feet" are talented in baseball, they smell terrible. However, in the end all is well because he becomes the spokesperson for the foot deodorant that Stanley's father invents on his way to figuring out how to recycle sneakers. Because the foot deodorant smells a little like peaches, they name it Sploosh, "in honor" of Kate Barlow's spiced peaches, which probably saved both Stanley and Zero's lives. Another names-related irony is that when Stanley first comes upon the wrecked boat and sees the name *Mary Lou*, he imagines Mary Lou as a beautiful young girl out with her lover rather than as a donkey carrying sacks of onions. But either way, he is quite right in realizing that someone probably drowned on the very spot where he is likely to die of thirst.

And while nobody really believes the old "joke" about the family being cursed because of the actions of their "no-good-dirty-rotten-pig-stealing-great-great-grandfather," it is interesting that Stanley's father discovers the wonderful foot deodorant the very day after Stanley Yelnats, the great-great-grandson of Elya Yelnats, carries Hector Zeroni, the great-great-great-grandson of Madame Zeroni, to the top of a mountain where he brings him water from the cool spring and comforts him with the old-world lullaby passed down through both families.

While Sachar's 2006 sequel, *Small Steps*, is not the tour de force that *Holes* is, for someone studying names it is almost as interesting because nearly half of the characters create new names for themselves. The story is set in Austin, Texas, where Kaira DeLeon, formerly known as Kathy Spears, is a popular young singer coming to town for a big concert. Armpit, from Camp Green Lake, is the protagonist; he has gone from digging holes at Camp Green Lake to digging holes for the Raincreek Irrigation and Landscaping Company while also going to summer school. The book opens with his digging a trench along the side yard of a house belonging to a woman named Cherry Lane, who happens to be the mayor of Austin.

X-Ray is the other returning character from Camp Green Lake. He is so proud of his nickname that he has it on his vanity license plate, a disadvantage when the police come looking to question someone named X-Ray for selling counterfeit tickets to a rock concert. X-Ray meets his clients in the parking lot of the H-E-B supermarket, which readers learn is named after the founder, Howard E. Butt, who rightly figures that few people will buy their groceries at a store called Butt's.

Armpit is having a hard time getting away from his nickname, which people assume means that "out of all those nasty, sweaty guys [at Camp Green Lake], he smelled the worst!" (89). When Armpit makes arrangements to take Tatiana, a girl who makes his knees weak, to Kaira DeLeon's concert, her friends say such things as "He'll probably put his big, fat, sweaty arm around you." She changes her mind so that at the last minute, Armpit invites Ginny, a ten-year-old neighbor girl with cerebral palsy to go with him.

Through some pretty unlikely circumstances, Armpit and Ginny end up watching the show from backstage and, after the show, having ice cream with Kaira in her dressing room. Ginny whispers to Kaira that Armpit's name comes from some part of his body, and so Kaira teases him by calling him Knuckles, Elbow, Muscles, Toenail, Hands, and Fingers. Ginny promises that it isn't anyplace "nasty," and so Armpit finally tells Kaira his name when she agrees that she will touch whatever it is. This turns out to be a kind of intimate little pleasure.

A funnier part is when Kaira is singing one of her songs and from backstage Armpit mishears it and thinks she is singing his name instead of "I'm but . . ." in,

> These shoes, these jewels, this dress.
> A perfect picture of success.
> You would never guess . . .
> *I'm but* a damsel in distress.
> Save me. *I'm but* a damsel in distress. (118)

Later when they get to know each other and he asks her about the words, they have a good laugh. One night during a concert she actually sings "Save me, Armpit! A damsel in distress." Neither the audience nor the band notices (196), nor does Armpit because he is still at home in Texas, getting ready to come and hear her sing at her next concert in San Francisco. Sachar uses the incident to show the high point of Kaira's feelings toward Armpit.

Polly Horvath's *The Canning Season*

Polly Horvath uses names for creating a fanciful tone of exaggeration in *The Canning Season*, which won the 2003 National Book Award. This grand old spoof is the story of thirteen-year-old Ratchet and fourteen-year-old Harper, who one summer begin making new lives for themselves in the bear-filled woods of coastal Maine. They are staying in the old Menuto family home now occupied by twin sisters, Penpen and Tilly, who are in their nineties, but still make a passable living by gathering and canning the wild blueberries that grow on their land.

In a six-page prologue, Horvath uses two name-related incidents, one about the Pensacola Hunt Club and the other about how Ratchet got her name, to introduce readers to Ratchet's mother, Henriette. She is a depressed woman who sleeps a lot in the "small, gloomy sub-basement apartment" where Ratchet has grown up in Florida. Ratchet understands that her mother is worn out "from waiting tables at the Hunt Club and from cleaning other people's apartments." For as long as Ratchet can remember, her mother has talked about the Pensacola Hunt Club "with its horses, tennis, swimming, and sumptuous club-house" as if it were Heaven on Earth (4). Ratchet is comforted by the idea of there being a place as wonderful as the Pensacola Hunt Club even though her mother explains that she could never take Ratchet to the club because of "that thing" (an unsightly birthmark) on her shoulder blade, which would show if she wore a swimming suit. Ratchet grows up thinking that she is the one keeping her mother from belonging to the Pensacola Hunt Club. But on the next to the last page of the book, readers learn that Ratchet, who is now a middle-aged woman, has telephoned the Pensacola Hunt Club and learned that anyone can be a member. It was never up to Ratchet to get her mother accepted. Henriette was using the name of the Pensacola Hunt Club not to refer to the actual establishment but as a metaphor for all the things in life she wants but suspects she will never have.

Along with obsessing about Ratchet's birthmark, Henriette bemoans Ratchet's unfashionable name—"That was your father's fault" (5). Ratchet has never met her father because he "took a powder" shortly after Ratchet was born. Henriette tells Ratchet the story on the same day that she informs her that she is going away for the summer. After giving birth to her first (and only) baby, she is in a foul mood because of the pain and stress of the delivery and the fact that at the hospital she has been wheeled into a room with seven other new mothers. Naturally, she makes a fuss: "I mean, if I wanted to hang out with a bunch of other women I would have lived in a commune, right? I would have had my labor in some touchy-feely ashram" (6).

Workmen are fixing pipes in the only available private room, but to keep Henriette from distressing all the other new mothers, the nurses put her in with the workmen. She soon gets rid of them by throwing around "bits of placenta" (really chunks of cherry Jell-O from her dinner tray). They leave in such a hurry that they forget to take all their tools. At first, Henriette does not notice because she is arguing with Ratchet's father over what to name the baby.

I liked the name Eugenie, and your father kept saying, "STINKO. Let's name her STINKO," just to be funny. Can you imagine annoying me after the kind of day I'd had? Then he says, "Or how about FART? FART Clark!"
I'd say Yvonne, and he'd say Belch. He just wasn't listening, he was too busy being hilarious. That's when I saw the tool on the windowsill. "Who left that ratchet on the windowsill?" I asked, but of course he can't just answer the question. He has to argue. "No, it's not a ratchet, it's a lug wrench." Well, I knew a ratchet when I saw one. (7)

Henriette tires of the argument and so pretends to read. The father gets so mad that he starts to dump Henriette out the window, but fortunately a nurse intercedes, and then someone in the hall shouts that Havana cigars are being passed out in the waiting room and Mr. Clark dashes off. Before he gets back, a woman comes in to get the information for the birth certificate and Henriette grabs the form and gets the last word in the argument by writing "Ratchet! Ratchet! in the space for the first and middle names," and that, she concludes, is "how you became Ratchet Ratchet Clark." Then as almost a P.S. she adds, "Oh, and by the way, you're going to Maine tonight" to stay with Aunt Tilly and Aunt Penpen (8).

Ratchet, who didn't even know she had any relatives, is being sent on the train to spend the summer with two women who are "great-second cousins once removed," but for convenience are called Aunt Tilly and Aunt Penpen. Ratchet's mother explains that she herself had spent summers with Tilly and Penpen and she is sending Ratchet there because she's now old enough "to get some away-from-home experience"; plus it is the only place she can think of that won't cost money (9).

In a little names joke that Horvath may have been making only for herself, Tilly and Penpen's family name is Menuto, which sounds like Spanish *menudo*, soup made from tripe. Henriette and Ratchet are already at the train station when Henriette describes the twin sisters as having been already old when she spent summers with them. By now she imagines they are "casket-ready." Then she adds that "Penpen was kind of fat and happy-happy all the time, and Tilly looked like a sphincter" (10). "Like a what?" Ratchet asks, but the conductor is hurrying her up the steps of the train so fast that there's no answer.

Ratchet's ticket says Dairy, but her mother has told her that the aunts live past Dink or maybe it's past Delta. When Ratchet is picked up at the train station and climbs into the aunts' ancient Daimler, "all these 'D' names blurred in her mind" (12). It hardly matters because after a tortuous trip through the dark woods they arrive at a house named Glen Rosa that isn't close to any town, which, as they explain to Ratchet, may turn out to be a problem because if they die (and they've always planned to die together), there won't be anyone to help Ratchet.

Ratchet, Penpen, and Tilly have a couple of weeks to get acquainted before the fourth character, Harper, appears in the book. During these weeks, Ratchet observes that Penpen is the stronger of the two women and that Tilly drinks way too much. She learns how Tilly's "brief but oddly satisfying marriage" had been inspired by a lumberjack's daughter named Lilla, but who everyone called Lilla Vanilla because her skin was so milky white. Actually, Lilla bleached her skin "with buttermilk all summer, so that she always had a slightly sour smell" (46), which made Tilly think no one would want to come close to her, but actually "she was so well wanted that she was pregnant, or as we used to call it, in a pickle" (47). Her father set out to arrange a marriage and since "Lilla didn't know which of her many suitors was the father," she chose the banker's son because he seemed to have the most potential. Because of the pregnancy, everything had to be speeded up, but still the wedding "was the biggest thing to hit Dink since a logger rolled his truck" (50).

The grandness of it inspired Tilly to get engaged to Burl, a lumberjack who "was not too bright" (77). At the wedding ceremony, Tilly changes her mind about marrying Burl, giving as her excuse the ridiculous vow of love that he and his fellow lumberjacks have composed for the wedding. While Tilly becomes a runaway bride, Burl is convinced that they are actually married. He tries to gain back his respectability by joining the Catholic Church, even though he has to go clear to Delta to find a priest. And later, when he actually marries Thelma, a bartender at the local tavern who still resents Tilly, he is convinced that their children are "born in sin." As Tilly explains to Ratchet, the children would never have known that they were "illegitimate" if Thelma didn't keep pointing it out to them and calling them Technical Sin One, Technical Sin Two, and Technical Sin Three (78).

With Harper's arrival, Horvath presents a third example of a mother being less than wise about the naming of children. Harper arrives on the front porch of Glen Rosa with an obviously pregnant Miss Madison. The pregnant woman has mistaken Glen Rosa for the St. Cyr's Orphanage, which is more than ten miles up the road. She explains that Harper's mother took off when Harper was just a baby and so she has been stuck with raising Harper, but now that she is going to have a child of her own, she's heading up to Canada. It was a French Canadian who got her pregnant, and she's going to look for his mother, who seemed like a nice person. This is why she finds it necessary to bring Harper to St. Cyr's, where she's heard they will accept anyone—even a big girl like Harper.

The long and the short of the story is that Ratchet and Harper both end up staying with Tilly and Penpen, who eventually will the house to them in exchange for the promise that they will never sell it. The pregnant Miss Madison keeps popping back into the picture, each time making Harper think she is going to "re-adopt" her. The final stamp is put on the matter when for the third time Miss Madison brings Harper and her suitcase back to Glen Rosa, along with the new baby, who she introduces with

It's Harpertu.
    Harper too? Asked Penpen,
    Yeah, Harpertu. H-a-r-p-e-r-t-u. I liked it. Had kind of a foreign ring about it. It'll be kind of an exotic name to take up there to French Canada. And like I said, I wanted to do something kind of to remember Harper by because if I could've seen a way to, I would have taken her, too. She knows that, don't you, Harper? (154)

Years later, Harper goes off to Brunswick College to become a specialist in worms and organic farming, while Ratchet stays at Glen Rosa making it a productive farm. Harper comes back every summer to help during the hectic blueberry season. By the end of the book, Ratchet has married a doctor who mistakenly comes to the house thinking it is the old orphanage, and Harper has married and given birth to six daughters. Three of them, including baby Tutu, Tilly, and Penny, have inherited names from earlier characters in the book. Fortunately, everyone in both families loves blueberry muffins.

~

CHAPTER TWO

Names to Establish Tone and Mode: Robert Cormier and Francesca Lia Block

Robert Cormier and Francesca Lia Block are both recognized as authors whose books are milestones in moving the field of young adult literature into new levels of sophistication. In 1974 when the American Library Association's *Booklist* reviewed Robert Cormier's *The Chocolate War*, the editors put a black border around the review to lament the passing of the sense of optimism that had always been an expected element in books published for young readers. Cormier's writing is brutally honest and several of his books can accurately be described as tragedies. And even the ones that he says are "happy" are written in a somber tone. A contributing factor to the success of his serious realism is his careful choice of character names.

Fifteen years after Cormier shook up the world of young adult literature, Francesca Lia Block arrived on the scene with *Weetzie Bat*. Reviewers were not prescient enough to figure out an appropriate border, but they were prophetic in observing that here was an exciting new author who was throwing to the wind another of the old expectations about books published for young readers. Rather than trying to inspire teenagers that they should work hard to get into a "good" college and prepare for a "good" job, Block was more interested in an alternative, but real, world.

Reviewers described her tone as "mesmerizing," "slinkster-cool," "intoxicating," and "glittering." They all agreed that the characters were searching for love and happiness, but at least a couple of critics questioned whether it was the kind of happiness that would last "forever after."

In this chapter, we will explore how these two skilled authors create and use names in quite different ways for quite different purposes. Because Cormier and Block's bodies of fiction for young readers are so full and rich, we will provide a complete list of Cormier's books for young adults, and a partial list of Block's books (she is still writing) in the bibliography at the end of the book. Our hope is that after reading about some of our favorite examples of naming techniques, readers will turn to these authors' books and find other treasures.

Robert Cormier's *The Chocolate War*, *I Am the Cheese*, *After the First Death*, and *Heroes*

In 1979 we were fortunate to visit with Robert Cormier in preparation for writing an article about names and naming. At the time, Cormier's books for young adults consisted of *The Chocolate War*, *I Am the Cheese*, and *After the First Death*. Based on these books and the fact that his lifelong career had been as a newspaper reporter, we expected Cormier to answer our questions as would a rushed, overworked, and perhaps cynical newsman. Instead he answered so much like a poet that we entitled our article "The Poetry of Naming in Young Adult Books." The unidentified Cormier quotes in this chapter come from that article, which was published in the spring 1980 issue of *The ALAN Review* (Vol. 7:3, pp. 3–4, 31).

We will look first at *I Am the Cheese*, because just as we teach our students that the settings in books can be either *backdrop* or *integral*, we use *I Am the Cheese* to illustrate that names too can be such an integral part of a book that the story would not exist without them. The metaphor in the title of *I Am the Cheese* comes from the old nursery song, "The Farmer in the Dell." Farmer is the surname of a family of three: David and Louise Farmer and their fourteen-year-old son, Adam. Their former names were Anthony and Louise Delmonte and their son, Paul. Their new names have been chosen by a man they know as Grey, but who probably has "a thousand names" (114). He "sponsored" the family when they were assigned to the U.S. government's witness reestablishment program. Some eleven years later, when the father explains the situation to Adam, he speaks in a tone of anger and disgust: "Farmer for God's sake. Grey and his bunch come up with Farmer. White, American, Protestant, WASP" (132). The father is disgusted because he is Italian and his wife is Irish and they are both Catholic. Grey decides to keep the family in the northeastern part of the United States and to let them remain Catholic, mainly so they can "fit in" with their neighbors.

When Adam was two years old, his father, who worked as a newspaper reporter, uncovered documents and obtained information at the Statehouse in Albany that could "change a lot of lives irrevocably" (123). Adam was never told exactly what the information was, but he knows it has something to do with links between the government and organized crime, and that his father was in Washington, D.C., for a year testifying before a secret Senate committee. Cormier said about Mr. Grey's name that the color "was important to the texture of the man and to the story itself, but it's too easy and obvious a name and I kept thinking I would change it sometime but never did. Actually the name just stuck and seemed fitting after a while." In the story Adam explains, "There was something gray about him. His hair was gray. But more than that: to me, gray is a nothing color and that's how Mr. Grey seemed to me. Like nothing" (109).

An indication of Cormier's care is that he uses an *e* in the man's name, but an *a* when talking about the color. Another subtlety is the fact that Adam's mother is the only one who does not have to change her given name. She was Louise Nolan before she was married, Louise Delmonte during the first few years of her marriage, and then Louise Farmer after the change. At first we suspected Cormier of a slipup, but then we decided that he wanted to communicate that she mattered so little to Grey and his men that they did not bother to demand a new name. Later in the story when Adam is being interrogated, he is never asked about his mother, which is one of the clues that helps him realize that his questioner is interested only in uncovering the criminal information, not in helping Adam come to terms with her death.

Adam remembers the time she told him about "her special terrors—the Never Knows" (153). Giving her insecurities a name complete with capital letters provides Cormier with a way to illustrate the situation. Among her "Never Knows" are what might be happening when a strange woman glances at her in a grocery store, or when the doorbell rings, or when her husband is late getting home. She shudders to think what would happen if they ever dared to defy Mr. Grey, a man who with just a phone call has the power to totally change their lives.

He does exactly this when he calls the family and tells them to take a weekend vacation out of town because he is worried that their identity has been uncovered. The trip is actually a setup and when they climb out of their car to "stretch their legs" and look at the view, which extends almost to Canada, a car comes hurtling toward them, "metal flashing in the sun" (198). As it crashes into them, Adam flies through the air and sees his mother's misshapen body land on the hood of the car and slide off. He knows she is dead, but he is unsure of whether his father has been hit or has run into the woods. Adam sees some giant legs in gray pants coming towards him while a familiar, cold voice says about his father, "He'll never get away," and about his mother, "She's terminated. . . . Move fast. Remove her." About Adam, "The boy," he says, "check him. He may be useful. Fast now, fast" (202).

It is late in the book before readers learn this information, which comes out in one of the memories that is patiently being picked from Adam's mind by Brint, who at first both Adam and readers think is a psychiatrist helping a damaged boy to heal. But as time goes on Brint, whose name rhymes with *flint* and *glint*, reveals himself to be an interrogator working for the same side as Mr. Grey. Cormier said he chose the name to suggest someone "bloodless and cold."

The story unfolds along two tracks, switching back and forth between Adam's surreal imaginings and/or remembrances as he rides his bicycle around the hospital grounds and Brint's taped interviews. This unusual organization drops readers into the same plane of confusion as are Brint and Adam. At first, readers think the boy is fine, but they feel sorry for him because on a cold, October day, "not a Thomas Wolfe October of burning leaves and ghost winds" but a cold and dreary day, he is riding an old-fashioned bicycle on a seventy-mile trip to take a present to his father, who he thinks is in a hospital in Rutterburg, Vermont (1).

Adam keeps stopping and trying to telephone his girlfriend, Amy Hertz, but he can never get through to her. He confides, "It's ridiculous that her name is Hertz—she's probably heard a thousand car-rental jokes and I have vowed never to make one" (4). When Cormier mentions this kind of name play it is usually to show that his characters are in a good mood. One of Adam's fondest memories is sitting between his parents as a little kid in the front seat of the family car and asking if they can stop at "Orange Johnson's" (he meant Howard Johnson's). "They laughed and laughed and I felt safe and secure and surrounded by love" (40). Sometimes in the dark, even now, he will say "Orange Johnson" just to make himself feel good and safe again.

Another incident of name play that he remembers with happiness is when he and Amy were getting ready to pull one of her tricks (what she calls "numbers") at a wedding. As they watch the families arriving all dressed up and holding their children's hands, Adam (she usually calls him Ace) was touched. Amy must have read his mind because she turns to him and says, "Isn't that nice, Adam? I think it would be nice to be married someday and have kids running all over the house." To make sure readers interpret this correctly, Cormier explains, "She seldom called him Adam, only at tender moments" (173).

When Cormier chose Amy's surname he had in mind the meaning of "hurts," because he knew she would have the power to hurt Adam. As it turns out, she never does; however some readers have questioned this based on the fact that her telephone call to Adam from her fa-ther's office is one of the first "clues" that Brint pries from Adam's memories. Amy's father is the editor of the *Monument Times* and one day she telephones Adam to say that a visiting editor from the town of Rawlings, Pennsylvania, where Adam's family supposedly lived, has told her father that there has never been anyone by the name of Farmer living in Rawlings. Adam shrugs off what she says, at least to Amy, but the incident triggers Adam's decision to become a spy in his own family.

During his spying, he eavesdrops from the downstairs telephone on one of the weekly calls that his mother makes. He has always been told that they have no relatives, but he hears his mother sharing the trivi-alities of Adam's past week with an older-sounding woman named Martha. Adam also snoops in his father's locked desk and finds two dif-ferent birth certificates for himself. When Adam's father finally shares their story, Adam remembers how a small part of himself felt "isolated and alone." That part was not Adam Farmer, but Paul Delmonte. "I am Paul Delmonte, a voice whispered inside him. Paul Del-mon-tee. Then who is Adam Farmer? Where did he come from?" (123).

Early on in Brint's interrogations, he says to Adam, "Now tell me, should we discuss Paul Delmonte?" (18). Adam declines and the tape is filed away. A new chapter starts with Adam pedaling on a road and singing the old nursery rhyme "The Farmer in the Dell." He happily remembers his father singing all the verses of the song and picking Adam up and swinging him almost to the ceiling and then bringing him back down to his mother's lap and asking what other family has a "theme song tailor-made for them?"

Although his mother would say, "They didn't make up the song for us," she would still fall into the game and smile when Adam's father would look down at him and argue, "Who says they didn't make up the song for us? . . . Suppose our name was Smith?" Did you ever hear anybody singing 'Mr. Smith in the dell, Mr. Smith . . .'" (19–20).

Cormier told us that Adam's first name was implicit in the story, "a whimsical choice—Adam, birth, rebirth—but Farmer of course, was part of the whole." Cormier thought of it long after he had inserted "The Farmer in the Dell" song. He called it "serendipity, really, which I believe in. I am always finding things not looked for."

These happy and loving scenes make the contrasting scenes about Adam's name all the more depressing. Tape number 7 is recorded in the middle of the night when Adam wakes up "as if shot out of a cannonball." He calls for Brint because he feels so isolated and alone, "caught and suspended" in time as he asks, "Who am I?" Adam Farmer is only a name, only words he has learned. "His name might as well have been Kitchen Chair. Or Cellar Steps. Adam Farmer was nothing—the void yawned ahead of him and behind him, with no constant to guide himself by. Who am I? Adam Farmer. Two words, that's all" (83).

Lines from the song are sung in various places throughout the book, but not until four pages from the end does Cormier include the last line of the song:

Heigh-ho, the merry-o,
The cheese stands alone. (210)

Earlier versions had stopped short by ending with "the rat takes the cheese." Either way, the line is an accurate description of what has happened to Adam. The last report that Brint files (number 16) is identified as the "third annual questioning of Subject A with results identical to two earlier sessions at twelve-month intervals." The writer recommends that "Subject A's confinement be continued until termination procedures are approved; or (b) Subject A's condition be sustained until Subject A obliterates" (213).

Cormier's Other Writings

The Chocolate War, which was Cormier's first book published for teen readers, is still his most famous. Although it is not as grim as *I Am the Cheese*, it was more shocking because in 1974 most teachers, librarians, parents, editors, and publishers subscribed to the idea that books for teens had to have happy endings. *The Chocolate War* is the story of Jerry Renault and his freshman year at Trinity High School. A corrupt Brother Leon is officially in charge of the school this year because the regular headmaster is ill, but the real "ruler" is a student, Archie Costello, and his obedient gang. The self-promoting Brother Leon orders twenty thousand boxes of leftover Mother's Day chocolates for resale, twice as many as the school has ever sold before.

One of the ways that Archie and his gang "rule" the school is by making "assignments" to younger, more innocent students. Brother Leon makes an unspoken quid pro quo arrangement to the effect that if Archie will encourage and help with the selling of the chocolates, Brother Leon will turn a blind eye to the actions of the Vigils. Archie, who masterminds the "assignments" that the Vigils give to younger and vulnerable students, decides to play with Brother Leon by choosing a student and telling him to refuse to sell the chocolates. He chooses Jerry Renault, a fourteen-year-old freshman whose mother has recently died and whose father is sleepwalking through life. The first few days Jerry hates refusing, but then he begins to savor his role of underground hero. When Archie tells him that the ten days are up, Jerry continues to refuse to sell the chocolates and in the end Archie arranges for a public boxing match between Jerry and a bully who administers a terrible beating in hopes of earning acceptance into the Vigils.

When talking about the names in the book, Cormier said that he loves contrasts—sharp ones—in both his characters' names and in the titles of his books; for example, the sweet *Chocolate* and the devastating *War*. He chose harsh, hard sounds for the names of villains like Archie and softer sounds for the name of someone like Jerry. When he named Brother Leon, he was looking for "a bland soft name to contrast with Archie because Leon was a bland-appearing man. And so is evil bland in its many disguises." Obie, the boy who handles all the details for Archie, "was a stooge with a stooge's name." Cormier said it reminded him of *obit*, the newspaper diminutive for *obituary*, but he added, "I grew to have compassion for Obie—he is to me a tragic character."

Cormier did not believe in consulting dictionaries or telephone books to find names; instead he simply thought about his characters for a long time before he put anything on paper. And when he started writing, the names were often lying there in his subconscious waiting to spring to life. The symbolism sometimes went from his subconscious to the reader's subconscious without either of them being fully aware of what was happening. For example, because we envisioned Archie basking in the glow of his fellow students' admiration, we asked Cormier if he had named the Vigils after the devotional candles that are placed at religious shrines. He said that he chose the name as a clipped version of *vigilante*, but in looking back at the book he realized that the devotional aspect of vigils was what made the name seem "so right."

Another question we asked was if he chose Archie as a name for his villain because of its dictionary meanings of "principal or chief as in arch-villain." He responded that Archie's name was one of those that just leaped into being as a good name for a villain, although ironically one of his longtime friends has the name. And when he first learned that Cary Grant's real name was Archibald Leach, he remembered thinking, "Archie, Archie Leach, what a contrast to what he was. And honestly, I think that had a lot to do with the selection of that name for my arch villain: the other side of Cary Grant, the other side of the coin."

Perhaps the most unusual use of names in *The Chocolate War* is when Cormier builds tension through creating a kind of daily names poem in which Brother Leon calls the roll, first asking the students to commit to selling the chocolates and then having them report on how many boxes they have sold since the day before. Chapter 13, which is about one-third of the way into the book, begins with Brother Leon calling:

> "ADAMO?"
> "Yes."
> "Beauvais?"
> "Yes."
> "Crane?"
> "Yo." Crane, the comedian. Never a straight answer.
> "Caroni?"
> "Yes."
> Everyone could see that Brother Leon was enjoying himself. This is what he liked—to be in command and everything going smoothly. The students responding to their names smartly, accepting the chocolates, showing school spirit. (79)

Between chapters 13 and 29, Cormier includes some fifteen of these little exchanges that readers, like the students in Brother Leon's class, begin to anticipate. They stand out because of providing white space on fairly dense pages. And as variations on a theme, they are fun to read because in each one Father Leon is somehow "bested" either by Jerry's refusal to sell the chocolates or by the other students "catching" Jerry's rebellious spirit.

Cormier's *After the First Death* was ahead of its time in 1979 when it told a story about terrorists from the Middle East who hijack a suburban school bus filled with first graders and driven by eighteen-year-old Kate Forrester. The person assigned by the U.S. military to solve the problem is General Mark Marchand. For his name, Cormier relied on "the harsh *Mark* and the soft *Marchand* . . . because we are all made of shares of softnesses and hardnesses."

Cormier chose Ben as the name of General Marchand's son, who is sacrificed in the story. Cormier said he had felt a bond to the haunting, evocative powers of the name ever since Thomas Wolfe mourned the death of his brother Ben. This contrasts with his choice of names for background characters who are more important for the role they play than for being unique personalities. Much like he chose Grey for the name of the government agent in *I Am the Cheese*, he chose the "fairly obvious" name of Stroll for a similar character in *After the First Death*, where he needed a name that would suggest coolness and casualness even during difficult times.

The two terrorists have a relationship that might make today's readers think of John Allen Muhammad and his teenage accomplice, Lee Boyd Malvo, who in the fall of 2002 were known as the "D.C. Snipers." Cormier named the leader Artkin and the boy he was working with Miro. When we asked if Miro was to suggest that the boy was a *mirror* image of Artkin, Cormier said that Miro "was simply the boy's name from the beginning." He wanted names that suggested the Mideast, but weren't actually, such as Artkin and Antibbe. When he realized that Miro sounded more Spanish than Arabic, he created a scene in a restaurant to justify Miro's choice of the name. Artkin asks Miro to tell him his "real name." Miro immediately recognizes this as a test and insists that his real name is Miro Shantas. He has no "fake name" (20). Artkin keeps pursuing the question, but Miro stands firm:

> He had not thought of his real name for such a long time that he had to dig back into his memory for it. Do not simply forget your name but bury it, the instructor had said. Bury it so that it never betrays you. Choose a name that is unlike your own or even the place of your origin. You must carry nothing with you that may betray you and that includes your name most of all. (21)

When a young waitress approaches the two men Artkin tells her, "That will be all, Myra." She responds with "My name's not Myra." Artkin smiles and agrees, "Of course it isn't." However "his voice suggested the opposite, his voice and his smile. They hinted wickedly of deep secrets." Even after she explains that her name is Bonnie and that is how she was baptized, "although the priest didn't like it because there is no Saint Bonnie," Artkin continues to call her Myra (22).

> Think about it, Myra. How old were you when you were baptized? Two weeks, two months? Do you remember being baptized with the name Bonnie? Of course not. It's what people have told you. Have you ever seen your birth certificate? Not the thing they give you when you go to City Hall for a copy, but the original? The one that says your name is Myra. You've never seen it, have you? But that doesn't mean it does not

exist. You have never seen me before but I exist. I have existed all this time. I might have been there when you were baptized, Myra. (22–23)

Before the girl flings the check on the table and leaves muttering "You're nuts," she stands in front of Arkin "the check in her hand, hesitant, doubtful, her eyes wary, and Miro knew that this was what Artkin had worked to do: create this split second of doubt and hesitation." As the moment vanishes, Artkin meets Miro's eyes and gives him "as much of a smile as he ever allowed himself" (23).

As is typical with Cormier, the scene serves more than one purpose. Besides justifying Miro's name, it demonstrates the slipperiness of the concept of "names" and their relation to people's inner psyches. It also reveals Arkin's confidence and his ability to manipulate people and make them question even their most basic beliefs about themselves and the world around them, and because the scene comes early in the book it prepares readers to appreciate Arkin's motivation and skill in the coming ordeal.

We will end this part on Cormier by looking briefly at one of his books written nearly twenty-five years after he wrote *The Chocolate War*. His 1998 *Heroes* begins with "My name is Francis Joseph Cassavant and I have just returned to Frenchtown in Monument and the war is over and I have no face." Francis is a wounded veteran, only eighteen years old. He alters his birth certificate and joins the army because he is looking for a way to die that will be more acceptable than jumping from the bell tower of St. Jude's Church. He wants to commit suicide because he is brokenhearted and ashamed of failing to protect Nicole Renard, the girl he has loved since seventh grade, from being raped by the hometown hero. Larry LaSalle is this hero, who comes home on a furlough to be honored by the citizens of Monument under his new title of "Lieutenant Lawrence LaSalle, U.S. Marine Corps, holder of the Silver Star for acts of heroism" (86).

Francis feels responsible because after the celebration he leaves Nicole in the town recreation center when she has hinted that he should stay, while Larry, who used to be their recreation director, has told Francis to go on home. Francis does not leave the building but neither does he make his presence known until it is too late. Francis expects to end his misery by falling on a grenade that is thrown at his platoon in an alley in

France, but instead he too wins a "Silver Star for an act of heroism" and in the process loses his face. He now wears a white scarf over the lower part of his face, and a Red Sox cap with the bill pulled so low that even the woman in the neighborhood that he used to run errands for does not recognize him. When he rents a room from her, she writes "Tenant" on the receipt. Later when she brings up a pot of soup she has made for him, she turns and says,

> "You didn't say your name." Not quite an accusation but as if her feelings have been hurt.
> Here is the point where my life becomes a lie.
> "Raymond," I tell her, using the name of my dead brother. "Beaumont," I add. My mother's name before she married my father. (25)

Francis does not want anyone to know who he is because as soon as he finds and kills Larry he plans to also kill himself and it is just as well that he be anonymous.

Heroes is only 135 pages long. One of the ways that Cormier achieves such efficiency is by dropping in the names of well-known people and leaving it to his readers to fill in the details he only alludes to. For example, as a preface he sets the tone of the book by quoting F. Scott Fitzgerald:

> Show me a hero and I will write you a tragedy.

Readers get a powerful visual image when Francis arrives back in town and describes himself as "the Hunchback of Notre Dame, my face like a gargoyle and the duffel bag [where he keeps his gun] like a lump on my back" (4). He reveals his attitudes towards his surgeon, Dr. Abrams, by describing him as being tall and looking "like Abraham Lincoln." His friend Enrico says that Dr. Abrams "should practice his cosmetic surgery on himself" (9).

When Francis is in London before his injury, readers get a glimpse into his personality through his complaining about its being a bright, sunny day. In his mind, London has always been linked "with foggy days and evenings and either Jack the Ripper or Sherlock Holmes stalking through the shadows" (83). Francis heads for Baker Street hoping to find 221B, even though he knows it is an address existing only in Conan Doyle's stories.

Earlier in Monument, when the old abandoned Grenier's Hall is turned into the Recreation Center that Larry LaSalle will manage, Eugene Rouleau, "the barber whose tongue is as sharp as his razor," observes that the whole remodeling process was "like watching a Marx Brothers movie" (40). It nevertheless becomes the means through which Larry LaSalle with his "Fred Astaire strut" (49) becomes "a bright Pied Piper" for the children of Monument during "the bleakness of the Depression" (87). One of the few other highlights from these terrible times was the mysterious stranger who came to town one summer and in the ball games in Cartier's Field would hit a home run in nearly every game. Many thought he "was a major league player in disguise. Babe Ruth, maybe, or Lou Gehrig" (50).

Thanks to Larry LaSalle, Francis becomes the table tennis—not the Ping-Pong—champion at what everyone calls the WRECK Center. This is on a Saturday, and the next day on Sunday Nicole Renard is to be the star of the musical show *Follies and Fancies*. Nicole invites Francis to a party she is hosting after the show at her house because "Larry says that's what people in show business do." Her words fill Francis with

> both delight and agony, delight at her invitation and the instant agony of jealousy, the way she had causally said his name—not Larry LaSalle or Mr. LaSalle, as all the kids referred to him, but Larry, spoken offhand as if they were more than teacher and pupil. (62)

The next day is Sunday December 7, 1941, the day of the attack on Pearl Harbor and the end of life in Monument as everyone knows it. Larry LaSalle goes off to war and the WRECK Center is closed "for the duration." However, it is reopened for the one night when Larry LaSalle comes home to a hero's welcome and to the events that change all three lives: Nicole's, Larry's, and Francis's.

Now upstairs in the room he has rented to stay in while waiting for Larry LaSalle to come home, Francis can never trace the moment when he finally falls asleep. While waiting he silently recites the names of the guys in his platoon—

> Richards and Eisenberg and Chambers and, yes, Smith—and their first names or nicknames—Eddie and Erwin and Blinky and Jack. Then, more last names, Johnson and Orlandi and Reilly and O'Brien and *their* first names, Henry and Sonny and Spooks and Billy—and then start all over again, arranging them this time in alphabetical order, still waiting for sleep to come. (28)

He doesn't want to think about them or about what happens when the grenade comes, but "every night the recitation begins, like a litany, the names of the GIs like beads on a rosary" (28).

The book ends with Francis again reciting the names of former soldiers, but not so fast and not with such rhythm. Now he thinks of "Enrico minus his legs and his arm" and of "Arthur Rivier, drunk and mournful that night in the alley" and he thinks that maybe he should "try to find Dr. Abrams' telephone number in Kansas City" (134). He is in a railroad station in the town where he has come to talk to Nicole about her new life. He has not killed Larry LaSalle—Larry saved him the trouble by shooting himself—and now that Francis is getting ready to leave, he picks up the duffel bag and slings it over his shoulder. Even though it still has the gun in it, "the weight is nice and comfortable" as he crosses "the lobby, heading for the exit and the next train to leave the station" (135).

Francesca Lia Block's *Weetzie Bat, Witch Baby, Cherokee Bat and the Goat Guys, Missing Angel Juan, Baby Be-Bop,* and *Necklace of Kisses*

There are officially five books in the set (*Weetzie Bat*, 1989; *Witch Baby*, 1991; *Cherokee Bat and the Goat Guys*, 1992; *Missing Angel Juan*, 1993; and *Baby Be-Bop*, 1995), but it is hard to say if and when the series really ends because in 2005 HarperCollins published a Francesca Lia Block book entitled *Necklace of Kisses*, which begins with "Where were the kisses? Weetzie Bat wondered." After almost twenty years, Weetzie's relationship with My Secret Agent Lover Man, who is now known as Max, has withered and so Weetzie leaves. Although the book was published by the adult division of the company, supposedly for women with fond memories of reading the Weetzie Bat books when they were teenagers, it was for sale at the 2006 convention of the Children's Literature Association in Mission Beach, California. The bookseller laughingly assured customers that teen readers were buying the book after going straight through the original Weetzie Bat books, now published in a single volume titled *Dangerous Angels: The Weetzie Bat Books* (1998). She was also offering for sale three reprintings put out by HarperCollins. Besides the original *Weetzie Bat*, she had a book entitled *Goat Girls* (2004), which includes *Witch Baby* and *Cherokee Bat and the Goat Guys*, and another one entitled *Beautiful Boys* (2004), which includes *Missing Angel Juan* and *Baby Be-Bop*. Except for *Baby Be-Bop*, the page numbers in this chapter refer to the books published as singles.

In the literary sense of the word, Block's stories are in the comic, rather than the tragic, mode. They start with something resembling normality followed by a period of chaos, which by the end rights itself to a kind of stasis. Block's tone is exaggerated and in keeping with her Hollywood setting, the genre is the kind of magical realism more often seen in film than in books. Charlie Bat, Weetzie's father, prepares readers for this by explaining why he cannot live in Hollywood:

> Everything's an illusion; that's the whole thing about it—illusion, imitation, a mirage. Pagodas and palaces and skies, blondes and stars. It makes me too sad. It's like having a good dream. You know you are going to wake up. (89)

In contrast to Cormier, who makes his stories so "realistic" that he can identify for readers the actual people whose names he borrows for his main characters, Block uses actual place names and the names of celebrities to establish her settings, but for her main characters she creates names that few people in real life are likely to have. The first two pages of the *Weetzie Bat* chapter entitled "Shangri-L.A." present an extreme example of how important names are to Block's writing. These pages contain 203 words, 71 of which (35 percent) are names, some appearing more than once. Character names include Weetzie, My Secret Agent Lover Man, Dirk, Duck, Cherokee, and Witch Baby. Names of their pets are Slinkster Dog, Go-Go Girl, Pee Wee, Wee

Wee, Teenie Wee, Tiki Tee, and Tee Pee. Actual names taken from the Los Angeles area include Hollywood Boulevard, Tick Tock Tea Room, Fredericks of Hollywood, Loves, Shangri-la, Shangri Los Angeles, Shangri-L.A., and Hollywood. Seasonal names include Christmas and October, celebrity names include Marilyn, Elvis, James Dean, Charlie Chaplin, Harpo, Bogart, and Garbo, while the one literary name is *Lost Horizons.*

The book begins with Weetzie explaining that she hates high school because her fellow students don't even care that Grauman's theater with "Marilyn's prints" is practically in their backyards or that they can buy "tomahawks and plastic palm tree wallets at Farmer's Market" and a wonderfully cheap lunch at Oki Dogs, and that the waitresses wear roller skates "at the Jetson-style Tiny Naylor's" (1). Both Jim Morrison and Houdini used to have homes in a nearby canyon, and "not too far away was Venice, with columns, and canals, even, like the real Venice but maybe cooler because of the surfers" (2).

Then Weetzie meets Dirk, a boy who not only "cares," but wears "his hair in a shoe-polish-black Mohawk" and drives a red '55 Pontiac, which Weetzie thinks "is the most slinkster-cool car" she has ever seen (3). Dirk has named his car Jerry (after Jerry Lewis) and at least partly because Jerry likes Weetzie, Dirk takes her to shows at the Starwood, the Whiskey, the Vex, and Cathay de Grande. In the daytime they go to matinees on Hollywood Boulevard and eat strawberry sundaes with marshmallow topping at Schwab's.

Block gives all of these details before she mentions that Dirk and Weetzie and Slinkster Dog spend lots of time at Dirk's Grandma Fifi's cottage "where Dirk had lived since his parents died" (5). The first mention of Weetzie's family is that her mom, Brandy-Lynn, dishes out weird meat for Slinkster Dog, who prefers eating pizza. For teenagers eager to get away from parental control, this sounds like a dream romance, but then at the end of the first chapter, Dirk tells Weetzie that he's gay. Weetzie gives him a hug and says, "It doesn't matter one bit, honey-honey. . . . Now we can Duck hunt together" (8–9).

By Duck hunting, Weetzie means looking for their true loves, which is what they do in chapter 2. Weetzie first goes home with a singer named Buzz, who turns out not to be a Duck but a "wild vulture bird" (11). She also meets a "Gloom-Doom Duck Poet," a "toothy blond Surf

Duck," and "an Alcoholic Art Duck with a pony-tail who talked constantly about his girlfriend who had died" (14). Dirk's luck is not much better, and the chapter ends with Weetzie saying, "I just want My Secret Agent Lover Man."

In chapter 3, readers meet Charlie Bat, Weetzie's father, who comes to visit from New York, where he is a writer of serious plays, not the kind of "Hollywood bullshit" he was writing when he met and accidentally impregnated Brandy-Lynn, Weetzie's starlet mother. In the next chapter, Grandma Fifi sees how sad Weetzie and Dirk are, and she gives an old lamp to Weetzie, who of course polishes it and then is amazed when a genie pops out and offers her three wishes. She wishes that Dirk will find his Duck, that she will find her own "My Secret Agent Lover Man," and that they can find a "a beautiful little house . . . to live in happily ever after" (28). Even before she can call Dirk to tell him about the genie, he calls to tell her that Grandma Fifi has died and has left them the house, including all the beautiful retro dresses that Weetzie loves. Weetzie's emotions go back and forth between sadness for Grandma Fifi's death and amazement at the circumstances.

In the next chapter, Dirk meets "the perfect Duck. But what is so weird is that this Duck calls himself Duck" (32). "Lanky Lizards!" is all that Weetzie can say. In the next chapter she is even more surprised when she is waitressing on a Sunday morning at Duke's and a man shakes hands and says, "I'd like to put you in my film. My Secret Agent Lover Man" (40). Weetzie at first thinks he has mistaken her for a boy, but he explains that "My Secret Agent Lover Man" is his name.

"Your name!" she shrieked.
"Yeah. I know it's a little weird."
"Dirk put you up to this."
"Who's Dirk?" (40–41)

"Lanky Lizards!" says Weetzie as she excuses herself and goes back to work. But in true fairy tale style, the man keeps coming back, and sure enough, becomes Weetzie's lover. Years have gone by, and the Jetson-style Tiny Naylor's drive-in (the place with the waitresses on roller skates) has been torn down and replaced with a record-video store, a pizza place, a cookie place, a Wendy's, and a Penguin's Yogurt. It is unclear whether these are simultaneous or sequential replacements, but what is clear is that Weetzie wants a baby. My Secret Agent Lover Man thinks, "There are way too many babies. And diseases. And nuclear accidents. And crazy psychos. We can't have a baby" (50). As an alternative, he brings home a puppy named Go-Go Girl so that when she grows up she and Slinkster Dog can have as many babies as Weetzie wants. Weetzie thanks him and hugs Go-Go Girl, but says she isn't the same as a real baby. By now, My Secret Agent Lover Man, with help from Weetzie, Dirk, and Duck, has made three movies and also some money. Dirk and Duck offer to have a baby with Weetzie. They all get medical tests, and when good results come back, Weetzie, Dirk, and Duck go out to celebrate their decision. In typical Block fashion, the readers are told what the three of them ate and drank: "hamachi, anago, maguro, ebi, tako, kappa maki, and Kirin beer," but very little about how Weetzie climbs in bed between Dirk and Duck to make the baby (55). My Secret Agent Lover Man is so angry about being left out of this decision that he leaves and Weetzie has a very long pregnancy because she is waiting not just for the baby but also for My Secret Agent Lover Man to come back.

The baby comes first, and so it is up to Dirk and Duck and Weetzie to name her. They had thought about Sweet and Fifi and Duckling and Hamachi and Teddi and Lambi, but they decide to name her Cherokee, because Weetzie, as she has pointed out at the very beginning, is "into Indians. They were here first and we treated them like shit" (3).

At last, My Secret Agent Lover Man comes back, soon followed by another baby girl—one that he fathered while he was away and became involved with a woman named Vixanne (Weetzie calls her Vixen) Wigg. She is in a Jayne Mansfield fan club and a witch's coven. She takes money from My Secret Agent Lover Man to have an abortion, but instead, she has the baby and leaves it on the doorstep. Weetzie wants to name the baby Lily and raise her as Cherokee's sister. Eventually everyone agrees, but all through the decision-making process, they refer to her as Witch Baby, a name that sticks and probably contributes to the identity problems that Witch Baby struggles with in the later books, when she and Cherokee are old enough to go looking for their own true loves.

In the second book, *Witch Baby*, readers learn that Dirk's family name is McDonald, while Duck's is Drake. Duck's siblings are named

Peace, Granola, Crystal, Chi, Aura, Tahini, and Yin and Yang—they're twins. Other characters who begin to take more important roles in this story of a truly extended family include Coyote Dream Song, an older Native American who lives on a hill in one of the canyons, the multiracial Jah-Love family consisting of a mother named Valentine, a father named Ping Chong, and their son named Raphael Chong Jah-Love. Raphael looks like powdered chocolate with eyes that remind Witch Baby of Hershey's kisses. Witch Baby, who all her life has taken out her frustration by pounding on things, is now a skilled drummer. She teaches Raphael to be a drummer and is brokenhearted when he uses his new skills to woo Cherokee. Another boy who Witch Baby connects with is Angel Juan, whose parents are Gabriela and Marquez Perez. He has two brothers named Angel Miguel and Angel Pedro and two sisters named Angelina and Serafina. Toward the end of the book, the family returns to Mexico and Witch Baby is left only with memories of Angel Juan and hopes for reconnecting in the future.

Witch Baby is basically unhappy in this book and does not see any angels in Los Angeles, a town that she thinks should be more accurately named Los Diablos (12) or Devil City. Throughout the book, she is given new names depending on what she is doing. In one of the happier parts when she is jamming on the drums with Angel Juan, he gives her the name of Bongo Baby as they make up songs entitled "Tijuana Surf," "Witch Baby Wiggle," and "Rocket Angel" (70). In a less happy part, Witch Baby hides in the trunk of Dirk and Duck's car when they go to visit Duck's family. The two had not planned to tell Duck's family that they are lovers, but much to everyone's shock, Witch Baby blurts it out and the three of them leave in a less-than-happy mood. However, near the end of the book, Duck's mom thanks her and says, "Without you, Miss Pancake Dancer Stowawitch, we might never have really known each other" (110).

In an attempt to help Witch Baby feel better about herself, Weetzie and My Secret Agent Lover Man tell Witch Baby that she truly is the daughter of My Secret Agent Lover Man. Witch Baby is thrilled to at last be ahead of Cherokee in knowing who her one "real" father is while Cherokee can only guess between Dirk, Duck, and My Secret Agent Lover Man. The strength of Witch Baby's bad feelings come out when she teases Cherokee and calls her Cherokee Brat Bath Mat Bat.

The third book, *Cherokee Bat and the Goat Guys* (1992), has a Native American connection in keeping with Cherokee's name. Cherokee and Witch Baby are older now and are left at home while Duck, Dirk, Weetzie, My Secret Agent Lover Man, and Raphael's parents go to South America to make a movie. Coyote Dream Song has promised to look after them, but he lives out in one of the canyons, and so basically, the girls, along with Raphael Jah-Love and Angel Juan, who has come back from Mexico without his family, are left to their own devices. They form a band called the Goat Guys. The chapter titles, "Wings," "Haunches," "Horns," "Hooves," and "Home," are each preceded by a Native American "poem" as well as a brief letter reporting on developments at home.

In "Wings," Cherokee uses real feathers that blow onto Coyote's hill to make a glimmering set of wings for Witch Baby. In "Haunches," she transforms a pair of jeans into goat pants for Raphael by sewing on the long strands of wool that Coyote clips from the haunches of his goats. In "Horns," Cherokee asks Coyote if she can give the goat horns that he has at his house to Angel Juan. When he says "No," Witch Baby sneaks in and steals them. Then in the next-to-the-last chapter someone leaves some "totally cool" hoof boots for Cherokee. Wearing these props when they perform gives them confidence and a unique appearance, but the more successful the band becomes, the less control the players have over their lives. Finally, Witch Baby goes to Coyote to ask for help, and he sends word to the parents that they are needed at home. He also conducts a healing circle that begins with

> "First we will all say our names so that our ancestor spirits will come and join us."
> "Angel Juan Perez."
> "Witch Baby Wigg Bat."
> "Raphael Chong Jah-Love."
> "Cherokee Bat."
> "Coyote Dream Song." (108–9)

Coyote chants and plays his drum and leads them in the sacred dances until they are all exhausted and sit leaning against each other feeling a new kind of protection and closeness. When Cherokee expresses her worries to Raphael about competing with the groupies who have been hanging around the band, Raphael reassures her with "You are my beauty, White Dawn" (106). By the time their parents get home, they are ready to work for a new start in the music business and are happy to find that minus the props, the alcohol, and the drugs, Raphael and Angel Juan can still "pout and gallop and butt the air," while on the drums Witch Baby can "hover, gossamer, above her seat" and a singing Cherokee can send "her rhythms into the canyon" (116).

The fourth book, *Missing Angel Juan*, is told from the viewpoint of Witch Baby, who is brokenhearted because Angel Juan decides that he needs to go to New York to see if he can make it on his own. Block uses several pleasant naming incidents to introduce the couple and their relationship, so that when Angel Juan leaves for New York readers know and like the couple well enough to care what happens to them. One of their appealing quirks is the way they give names to whatever they happen to like. They call their Joshua tree cactus Sunbear, and when they sleep outside under the backyard lemon tree and wake up to the "yellow smell of lemons" (64) they name the birds that are singing in the leaves Hendrix, Joplin, Dylan, Iggy, Ziggy, and Marley. When Witch Baby fantasizes about having children with Angel Juan she thinks of "brown baby twins with curly cashew nut toes and purple eyes. Kid Niblett and Señorita Deedles" (81).

Angel Juan calls his true love "Niña Bruja or Baby or Lamb" (3) until on the night he tells her that he is going to New York; then he addresses her as Witch Baby. When this happens, she tears up the dozens of pictures she has taken of him. At school, she feels like she comes from another planet—"Planet of the Witch Babies where the sky is purple, the stars are cameras, the flowers are drums and all the boys look like Angel Juan" (13). As Christmas vacation approaches, Witch Baby tells her "almost mom" Weetzie Bat that she is going to New York to find Angel Juan. In her detective role, she calls herself Witch Baby Secret Agent Wigg Bat.

She has only the ten days of Christmas vacation in which to find him, and this is where the fairy tale aspects of the story come into play. Weetzie has kept her father's New York apartment since he died when Witch Baby and Cherokee were toddlers. Witch Baby is able to stay there, with the help of two elderly neighbors—Meadows and Mallard, who live downstairs and act like kindly fairy godfathers in providing her with food and a Persian rug to sleep on. Mallard is still wondering why, when Weetzie came to visit years earlier, she had thought his name was funny. Witch Baby doesn't know how to tell him that "in my family duck means a pounceable guy who likes guys, which is what Mallard is—a very grown-up gray duck," and so she settles on saying simply that "in my family names are a kind of weird thing" (33).

Grandfather Charlie comes out in his ghost form to lend guidance and moral support. His biggest contribution is the way he encourages Witch Baby to enlarge her vision and to look at some of the things in New York that she is missing by focusing only on clues to Angel Juan's whereabouts. One of his successes is when Witch Baby sees some little girls playing "hip-hop-hopscotch" to the music of their "ghetto blaster blasty blast." She takes pictures of these "mini fly-girls" doing "the Running Man and Roger Rabbit, Robocop and Typewriter in the chalk squares" (56). He also leads her—a "will-o'-the-wisp white child"—to hang for an hour with a fantastic group of African drummers who let her play with them because she is knowledgeable enough to know *Fanga, Kpanlogo, DunDunBa,* and *Kakilamba* (89).

Clues that she is getting nearer to Angel Juan include finding some of his carving on a tree house in Central Park, a discarded photo of him taken at a Coney Island booth, and a postcard addressed to her and signed "Yo Te Amo, Niña, Angel Juan" (93). When, with even more magical help, she finds Angel Juan, she has gained enough wisdom and understanding to offer him Grandpa Bat's apartment so that he can stay for as long as he needs to. As she bids a temporary farewell to him, she calls him "my black cashmere cat, my hummingbird-love, my mirror, my Ferris wheel, King Tut, Buddha Babe, marble boy-god. Just my friend" (137). He calls her Miss Genie because of the way she has managed to free them both from their fears.

The fifth book, *Baby Be-Bop* is basically the story of Dirk's growing up and realizing that he is gay. He remembers overhearing Grandma Fifi confide to her canaries, Pirouette and Minuet, that "it's hard for him without a man around" (164). She also has a cat named Kit who "is a great healer in a cat's body," and a dog named Kaboodle the Noodle "who has a valentine nose, long Greta Garbo lashes, and a tiny shock of hair that stood straight up" (168). Even as a boy, Dirk recognized that Grandma Fifi's gay friends, Martin and Merlin, were afraid and acted in a way he did not identify with. One of the reasons Dirk is so "slinkster-cool" is that all his life he has aspired to be different from the stereotypical view of wimpy, gay men. His dreams come out in a comic strip he draws about two boys named Slam and Jam, who turn into superheroes when problems need solving. All goes well until he and his best friend, Pup, become teens and Pup makes it very clear that he prefers girls. Dirk thinks about starting a band called the Tear Jerks. Thanks to the magic of Grandma Fifi's lamp, Dirk gets to know his family history and have a long conversation with his father, Dirby. Dirk's grandfather (Grandma Fifi's husband) was named Derwood, and when he married Fifi he knew that he was soon to die so he didn't even try to be a father to Dirby. When Dirby was sixteen and suffocating in his mother's sugar-sweet kitchen, he started hanging out at nightclubs and writing poetry. Because he was so young he was called Bo-Peep, but then when he read his poems, people changed his name to Be-Bop. He met Dirk's mother at a poetry reading. She was a "boyish goddess. . . Edie Sedgwick and Twiggy and Bowie and like his father she was James Dean too" (258). She introduces herself to Dirby by saying, "My name is Just Silver . . . Just Silver with a capital J capital S. The Just is because I renounced my father's name" (259).

Dirby and Just Silver love their new baby, but they are drawn "more and more into the waves and the wind" (263) and the night they "gave up on life," Dirby tells Dirk that

> I can't say it was a conscious decision. But we didn't struggle against it either. That was the year Martin Luther King and Robert Kennedy were killed. In a way I think it was all too much for us—this world. (264)

One of the last things that Dirk says in this conversation is "But I'm gay. . . . Dad, I'm gay." With his "lullaby eyes" singing with love and Just Silver dancing behind him, Dirby says, "I know you are, buddy," and then goes on to ask Dirk if he knows "about the Greek gods, probably Walt Whitman—first beat father, Oscar Wilde, Ginsberg, even, maybe your number one hero? You can't be afraid" (264). This acceptance by his parents is the climax of the book. The denouement is a final chapter entitled "Genie," which presents an abbreviated version of Duck's story.

CHAPTER THREE

~

Names to Establish Time Periods: Karen Cushman and Her Historical Fiction

According to language historian J. N. Hook, who wrote *Family Names: How Our Surnames Came to America*, most English and Continental surnames in the United States were developed during the Middle Ages. Since Hook wrote his book in the early 1980s, many non-European immigrants have come to the United States bringing with them their own naming customs, which means that not quite so many Americans can trace their names to the customs that Hook describes from the Middle Ages. Nevertheless, these customs are interesting in what they reveal about naming practices, and they are especially interesting in relation to Karen Cushman's two best-known books, *Catherine, Called Birdy*, and *The Midwife's Apprentice* (winner of the 1996 Newbery Award), which are set during the latter part of the Middle Ages.

As we read these books, we were struck not only by how much Cushman knows about naming practices of the Middle Ages, but also by how skillfully she uses these practices to keep her readers immersed in the time period. We will first write about the personal names in these two books set near the end of the thirteenth century and then will skip some 550 years ahead and look at Cushman's *The Ballad of Lucy Whipple*, which is set during the California Gold Rush in the mid-1800s. Our goal is to explore and compare the ways that Cushman uses names to frame two different time periods in two different parts of the world.

According to Hook, the Middle Ages was a time when few people traveled further than fifteen or twenty miles away from their birthplace, and so people were often given names that identified where their families lived. This kind of surname is now seen on Lauryn Hill, Earl Warren, Gwendolyn Brooks, Clint Eastwood, Winston Churchill, Tallulah Bankhead, Jeff Bridges, and Alan Greenspan. Another technique was for a family to be named after a characteristic of one of the family's leading members, as seen in such surnames as those belonging to Lance Armstrong, Loretta Young, John F. Long, Harry Truman, Vanna White, Ken Strong, David Lean, and Rita Mae Brown.

Other surnames came from the family's employment. People with the last names of Chandler and Wickman have ancestors who made candles; the ancestors of people named Arrowsmith or Fletcher worked with bows and arrows; while people named Sawyer or Carpenter have ancestors who were builders. Margaret Thatcher's ancestors (or rather the ancestors of her husband) were roofers; Peter Seller's ancestors were shopkeepers or peddlers, and Jimmy Carter's ancestors were in the business of moving or carting things from place to place.

The fourth way that surnames were decided on was for the children in a family to be given a surname taken from one of their parents. This was usually taken from the father as in such surnames as Johnson, Anderson, and Nilsen, but occasionally a family's name came from the mother's side of the family, as is thought to have happened with the name Marriot (child of Mary), Anson (son of Ann), and Tilson and Tillotson (son of Tillie or Matilda).

One reason that these four basic processes are not more universally recognized is that many of them occurred in non-English-speaking countries so that when immigrants brought their names into what became the United States, English speakers did not recognize the sources of the names. For example, an English person with the descriptive surname of Bigg or Bigler has a name that is semantically related to the French names of LeGrande, the Spanish name of Gordo or Gordon, the Italian name of Grosso, and the Hungarian name of Nagy. Patronyms (names from fathers) include McDonald (son of Donald in Irish or Scottish), Upjohn (son of John in Welsh), Janicek (son of Jan in Polish), Fitzpatrick (son of Patrick in Irish), Petroff/Petrovich (son of Peter in Russian), Antonopoulous (son of Antony) in Greek, ben Gurion (son of Gurion) in Hebrew, and D'Angelo (son of Angelo) in Italian. Another reason that the naming processes are not clearly transparent is that many of the prepositions and articles were in French because of William the Conqueror's success in 1066 when he conquered England and made French the official language so that *de* was used for "of" or "from," *le* for "the," and *atta* for "at." These, along with hyphens, gradually dropped away. Also, the orthographic idea of consistent capitalization and spelling is fairly recent.

In summary, people's surnames and, to a lesser extent, their given names were

1. Based on place names,
2. Described personal characteristics,
3. Described a person's occupation, or
4. Were patronyms based on the personal name of a father or another admired person.

Authors do not go about creating or choosing names to fit into these patterns, but the processes are so common that readers have grown accustomed to looking for relationships between people's names and their characteristics. This is even truer in literature than in real life, because readers know that authors have control over the names of their characters and so they expect that the name an author chooses or creates will reveal something about the role that the character will play in the story. It is less common to expect names to reveal something about the time period of a book, but as we will show in this chapter, names can go a long way toward establishing a time period, especially in historical fiction.

Surnames became necessary because the same given names were repeated over and over, and as people began to live in larger villages and trade with nearby villages, it became harder to know who was being referred to at a time when 17 percent of all men were named John, followed by William, Thomas, and Robert, and 5 percent of all women were named Alice and 4 percent Joan (with various spellings).

Naming Practices in *Catherine, Called Birdy* and *The Midwife's Apprentice*

In *Catherine, Called Birdy*, thirteen-year-old Catherine has been born into the family of a minor nobleman, who hopes to make a profit when he arranges her marriage. She is called Birdy because she is fond of keeping caged birds. She tells her story through writing a daily journal, as suggested by Edward, her brother, who is a monk and thinks that such writing will help her "grow less childish and more learned." Birdy scoffs at this idea, but nevertheless accepts the trade-off that her mother offers, which is that on the days that she writes in her journal, she will not have to spin wool. As Birdy confides to the reader, her mother is doing this "to please Edward" rather than because she is in favor of writing (2). The main conflict in the story comes from Catherine's father trying to arrange a profitable marriage for his teenage daughter, and Catherine's resistance to being "sold" to the highest bidder.

In *The Midwife's Apprentice*, an orphan girl variously called Brat, Dung Beetle, and sometimes just Beetle, has no idea of where or when she was born. Midway through the book, she decides to give herself the name of Alyce, which is how we will usually refer to her. The story starts on a cold morning when she is found by a village midwife while she is sleeping in a dung heap to take advantage of the naturally produced heat that results from decomposition. As she opens her eyes, the midwife Jane says, "Good. . . . You're not dead. No need to call the bailiff to cart you off. Now out of that heap and away" (3).

> The fierce pain in her stomach made Brat bold. "Please, may I have some'ut to eat first?"
> "No beggars in this village. Away." (4)

But then Jane smells the girl's "hunger, which she could use to her own greedy purpose," and tells the girl to get up and she will try to find her something to do (4).

Because the books come from opposite ends of the social scale, they provide a wonderful illustration of the four processes of naming that Hook outlines. All through the Middle Ages, the processes of naming were fluid with crossovers between given names and surnames. Only late in the period were children given the same surname as their parents, whether or not the name was still descriptive of their coloring, or employment, or where they lived, and so on. In the history of naming, this was a major step, but because governments were decentralized and there were few ways to communicate, the idea of inheriting one's surname did not come about all at the same time. And as shown through examples from Cushman's two books, it is not always clear whether a name is describing someone's appearance, their job, or a characteristic. For example, the owner of the tavern where Alyce works for a while after running away from the midwife is named John Dark "for he was nearly sightless, but none so blind that he could not find an untended mug of ale anywhere on the table or pinch a plump cheek as it passed" (74). If his name should become adopted as the surname of his descendants, within a few generations they probably would not know that their name traced to the fact that an ancestor was blind, rather than that he had dark skin or dark hair. Others of the names that Cushman uses to give a historical flavor to her books illustrate crossovers between first and last names. Even though there is considerable swirling among the categories, we are presenting examples from the two books roughly organized according to the four basic types of naming patterns that Hook describes.

Place Names

In *Catherine, Called Birdy*, people named after where they live include an old man named John Over-Bridge who hobbles so painfully that Katherine says, "I think God would not choose to be an old man" (156). A more fortunate villager is Henry Newhouse, who "at thirty acres" has "the largest holding" (8). At the opposite end of the social scale is Thomas Cotter, whose surname means "peasant" and is cognate with *cottage*. One of the suitors that Catherine's father tries courting for her is "the fat and flabby son of the baron Fulk from Normandy" (72). Another suitor never makes it to the manor because Catherine, who has volunteered to help mix the "mud, straw, cow hair, and dung into daub for covering the walls" of a newly built cottage greets him kindly as he approaches. He covers his nose with a "scent-drenched linen" handkerchief and asks for the manor of Rollo of Stonebridge. When she inquires of his business and he says it is to inspect "the family with an eye to marrying the daughter Catherine," she cleverly offers such disgusting "facts" about Catherine that the "beautiful horse with the beautiful young man left the road, made a wide turn in the field, trampling the carefully seeded furrows of Walter Mustard, and tore off away from the manor" (17). Instead of referring to her own home as Stonebridge, Catherine calls it the "old Spinning and Sewing Manor" (12).

In *The Midwife's Apprentice*, those who called Alyce Dung or Dung Beetle were using a kind of place name alluding to where Alyce most often slept. Or perhaps we should classify it as a descriptive name because it also says something about how Alyce smells or how she looks like a beetle curled up in such places. When the midwife ministers to villagers, she tells Alyce that she is taking "comfrey tonic to Joan At-the-Bridge" (18), and on the day that Alyce decides to run away from the midwife because she feels like a failure, she passes Alnoth the Saxon cleaning the manor privies and cursing "god for making him a peasant and not a lord" (70).

Names Descriptive of Personal Characteristics
Descriptive names in *Catherine, Called Birdy* include the name of Catherine's grandfather, Fulk Longsword; villager Robin Smallbone, and villager Ralph Littlemouse, who is a hero for throwing a bucket of water on a chicken whose feathers were on fire and in its frantic dash to outrun the fire was setting houses ablaze. When Catherine is considering taking up the cross and becoming a crusader, she talks about Richard the Lionheart and the terrible John Softsword. Perkin, the goatkeeper at the Manor, is chosen to be Lord of Misrule for the Christmas Revels. A kinsman of her mother who comes to spend Easter week with them "is called Odd William to distinguish him from William Steward and Brother William at the abbey" (95). When Catherine's father objects to sending wagons full of gifts to the abbey where Edward is a monk, Catherine's mother calls him Pinch-Fist and Miser. Catherine refers to her father as "the beast," or when she is being more formal, as Sir Nip Cheese. However, she saves her most interesting names for visitors to the manor, including a tiny, aging woman with little red eyes and only two top teeth, whom she names Madame Mouse. Among the names she chooses for the suitors her father invites to visit are Master Lack-Wit, Poor Fire Eyes (his eyes were on fire from greed), and Old Shaggy Beard.

Those who early in *The Midwife's Apprentice* refer to Alyce as Brat were using a descriptive name. Also, early in the book Alyce's mistress was known as Jane the Midwife, but very soon Alyce begins thinking of her as Jane Sharp "because of her sharp nose and sharp glance" (11). This is what Cushman calls her throughout the rest of the book because it aptly describes how she does her job:

> with energy and some skill, but without care, compassion or joy. She was the only midwife in the village. Taking Beetle gave her cheap labor and an apprentice too stupid and scared to be any competition. This suited the midwife. (11)

For weeks after Alyce was unable to help the miller's wife deliver her baby, the midwife called Alyce "not Beetle but Brainless Brat and Clod-pole and Good-for-Nothing" (24), which made Alyce work twice as hard and say only half as much because she did not want to have to leave.

An important part of the story happens after things calm down a bit and Alyce has time to wander in the village and watch and learn from a wood-carver, "old Gilbert Gray-Head," a man whose descendants probably have the surname of Gray. Alyce carves two mysterious little hooves and makes tracks with them, which the townspeople believe to be the Devil's tracks. After her carvings have done their mischief, she drops them in the river and several days later they wash up a few miles away where Annie Broadbeam puts them, in her cooking fire and en-joys "a hot rabbit stew on a cool autumn night" (47). Annie Broad-beam's descriptive name was probably later changed to something like Broadbent, while Thomas the Stutterer's last name was probably changed to something like Stutton or Stratton.

One of the few villagers in *The Midwife's Apprentice* to become al-most friends with Alyce is a boy with red hair named Will Russet (*rus-set* is the Old French word for "red"). When Alyce sees a newly born calf, which was "a sweet and sticky thing," she names it "Rosebud, for she was as red as the hedgeroses near the village church" (89).

Occupational Names

In *Catherine, Called Birdy*, occupational names are common because Catherine's family has several servants and each of the villagers must pay yearly rent to her father. On the day Catherine runs away with some Jewish refugees and ends up at a fair, she comes home with William Steward, a man she had earlier described as "William the Steward" (7). His surname traces back to "Keeper of the Sty," as in *pigsty*, but by the time of the story in 1290, the name had become more positive and was used for the "manager" of an estate. William was at the fair buying supplies for the manor. When William collects the rent from the villagers, Catherine always sits nearby and eavesdrops because she likes to hear them complain about her father. As she explains, "I have gotten all my good insults and best swear words that way" (7). Among those paying are Thomas and Ann Baker and Cob the Smith. Cuthman Cook works in the kitchens of the manor, while Thomas Carpenter works in the house and outbuildings. Catherine thinks of asking him to help her construct a trapdoor in the hall so she can drop her suitors into the river as they arrive.

There are relatively few occupational names in *The Midwife's Apprentice*, but that is probably because for most of the book Alyce knows few people. One of the men she passes when she makes her way to the Manor to check on an orphan boy is named Roger Mustard; since he is carrying a weed hook he is probably a mustard farmer. When Alyce finds an orphan boy and sends him to a nearby manor, he is more or less adopted by a woman the boy refers to as Cook, which in his mind is both her job and her name. In a way, Alyce gives her cat an occupational name. She offers him a whole string of names: Purslane? Gypsy Moth? Lentil? Bryone? Millstone? Fleecy? Earthpine? Dartmoor? Cheesemaker? Holly? Pork? Columbine? Cuttlefish? Clotweed? Shrovetied? and Wimble? All he does is sit there and purr and so she names him Purr.

Patronyms

The literal meaning of *patronym* is something like "father's name," but Hook considers the term more broadly so as to include being named "after" any specific person. In *Catherine, Called Birdy*, when a neighbor brings five puppies from their best hound as a gift, Catherine names the little male Brutus after the first king of Britain, while she gives plant names to the females. The most common patronymic names come from saints, a practice which for hundreds of years kept the body of English names fairly small.

Much of Catherine's humor comes from the way she plays with the names of saints. Her journal begins on September 12 in the Year of our Lord 1290. In the beginning, she has very little to say, reporting only on such details as how many fleas she has picked off or on whether or not she has tangled her sewing threads. But early in October she is allowed to travel to the abbey where her brother is a monk, helping to copy and bind great books. Her entry for October 13 begins with "Feast of Edward, king and saint, and my brother Edward's saint's day" (22). From here until the book ends on the twenty-third day of September 1291, Catherine starts each entry by identifying whose saint's day it is. Some sound genuine as with "18th Day of October, Feast of Saint Luke, writer of gospels, physician, and artist, who lived to be eighty-four and died unmarried" (25), but others were clearly invented for humor. The twenty-fifth of October is "Feast of Saints Crispin and Crispinian, shoemakers, pricked to death with cobblers' awls," while the twenty-sixth is "Feast of Saints Eata and Bean, which I think is very funny," and the third of November is "Feast of Saint Rumwald, who at three days old said 'I am a Christian' and died."

Cushman is a historian especially interested in correcting the gender imbalance in most history books. She worked hard to have Catherine include female as well as male saints and many of her sly comments may cause readers to ponder on such things as why on the seventeenth of October we hear only about the male side of the family: "Feasts of Saints Ethelred and Ethelbricht, sons of Ermenred, great-grandsons of Ethelbert, brothers of Ermenburga, nephews of Erconbert, and cousins of Egbert." The nineteenth of October is the "Feast of Saint Frideswide, virgin, though why that should make someone a saint I do not know," while the twentieth is the "Feast of Saint Irene, killed by a man because she would not love him," and the twenty-first is the "Feast of Saint Ursula and her eleven thousand companions, martyred by the Huns."

In *The Midwife's Apprentice*, Alyce gives herself a kind of patronymic name when at the St. Swithin's Day Fair at Gobnet-Under-Green she is mistaken for a girl named Alyce. She is allowed to go to the fair only because the midwife has fallen and broken her ankle and she needs someone to buy supplies for her. The girl has begged at fairs before but "never had her belly been full enough for her to lift her head and look around" (25). This time she has to interact with people to buy the things Joan Sharp needs. She has been told that she could get the best prices for leather flasks at the end of the Street of Cup Makers "just before the Church of Saints Dingad and Vigor. And so she did" (29). Perhaps because she is so new at bargaining, she handles "it with such charming solemnity" that the merchant takes a fancy to her and throws in a wooden comb (29). He also throws in a wink and a compliment: "Comb those long curls till they shine, girl, and sure you'll have a lover before nightfall" (30).

These two breathtaking events have just happened, when a man comes up thrusting a piece of paper at her and asking her to read the figures on it. This was in the days before common people were fitted with eyeglasses, and he thought she was someone named Alyce—a girl who could read. He finally realizes that she isn't the Alyce he is looking for, but he has lit a torch inside her.

"Alyce," she breathes. Alyce sounds clean and friendly and smart. You could love someone named Alyce. . . . "This then is me. Alyce." It was right (32).

When she gets back to the cottage and Joan Sharp tells her to get out of her sight "Dung Beetle, before I squash you" Alyce corrects her by saying "Alyce."

"What did you call me?"
"Not you, me. Alyce. My name is Alyce."
"Alyce!" The midwife snorted like Walter Smith's great black horse, Toby. (33)

And then in a line that is reminiscent of Humpty Dumpty in *Through the Looking Glass* where he tells Alice that "with a name like that, you could be almost anything," the midwife continues: "Alyce! You look more like a Toad or a Weasel or a Mudhen than an Alyce." And as she speaks she punctuates each name with another pot thrown in the girl's direction so that "Beetle thought to go out" (33).

The first baby that Alyce successfully delivers is named Alyce Little "in honor" of Alyce's help in the delivery. And when she meets an abandoned boy, who reminds her of herself before she was taken in by the midwife, he tells her his name is Runt. She immediately tells him that Runt is not a real name, and that to make his way in the world he must have a name. He says he will take her name, but she explains that's not possible because it is a girl's name. Then he says he will take the king's name and so she has to inquire of the village folk to find the name of the king:

"Longshanks," said the baker.
"Hammer," said Thomas At-the-Bridge.
"The Devil hisself," said Brian Tailor, who was a Scot and so had reason to feel that way.
"Just 'the king' is all," said several.
"Edward," said the bailiff. "The king's name is Edward."
"Edward," said Alyce to the boy.
"Then Edward is my name," said Edward, who used to be called Runt. Alyce nodded. (65)

In a kind of parody to the practice of naming humble creatures after great and famous people, when Alice helps deliver Tansy's twin calves, they get named Baldred and Billfrith "after the saintly local hermits" (62). When Alyce is called on to help deliver a baby for a noblewoman at the Tavern who had not even known that she was pregnant (she thought she had a stomach worm) Alyce calls "on all those saints known to watch over mothers—Saint Margaret and Saint Giles and Saint Felicitas, and even Saint Loy, who protects horses, and Saint Anthony, who does the same for pigs, for she believed it would do no harm" (109).

The Ballad of Lucy Whipple

The Ballad of Lucy Whipple begins in the summer of 1849 when its spunky heroine has just arrived in California, fallen down a hill, and vowed to be miserable. Her parents, who used to live in Butterfields, Massachusetts, had long dreamed of going West, even naming their children and the family dog, Rocky Flat, after their dream. The thirteen-year-old heroine is named California Morning Whipple, followed by her brother Butte, and her sisters six-year-old Prairie and four-year-old Sierra. The baby of the family, Golden Promise, has died from pneumonia along with the father in the autumn of 1848. The next to the youngest, who was named Ocean, disappeared in the Massachusetts woods when she was taking a walk with her mother.

After the deaths of the baby and the father, everyone tells Mrs. Whipple that she will have to give up her dream of going to California, but "after grieving for a spell over what was lost, she took a deep breath and started to look toward what was to come" (4) Butte, Prairie, and Sierra are excited, but California dreads it and has bad dreams, which continue when they are packed "up like barrels of lard" and put on a "ship with raggedy sails to seek our fortune in the goldfields of California" (4). When they get to San Francisco, they live on board the ship for eight days (the captain and the crew have all run off to the goldfields) while Mrs. Whipple stalks "through San Francisco in her black dress, new flowered hat on her head and a copy of *The Emigrant's Guide to the Gold Mines* . . . tucked in her reticule" (4). Mrs. Whipple gets an offer of a job running a boardinghouse (actually a tent) and the family—or what's left of it—trudge "three days through country jagged with hills and mountains, peaks and valleys, blazing sunshine and cool sharp nights" (4).

In chapter 2, California decides to change her name. Back home, it was

just a name, like Patience or Angus or Etta Mae. But in California it was not just a name. It was a place, a passion, a promise. It was a name that caused people to notice me, talk to me, remember and expect things. It was in no way the right name for me. (9)

Lucy first shares her new name with her Gram and Grampop in a letter explaining that California Morning Whipple is a foolish name "for a duck much less a girl. . . . I cannot hate California and be California," and so she hopes that they will understand and now address her as Lucy (13). Her brother, Butte, thinks that Lucy makes her "sound like some dainty showoff from the city. Lucy Belle. Lucy May. Lucy dearest," he snickers (35). Her mother responds to the new name with "After twelve years of calling you California, I don't see how I can suddenly say Lucy any more than I could Bossie or Nelly or Lady Jane." Lucy humbly asks, "Will you try, Mama?" (39). Finally, when her mother is desperate for an afternoon away from her duties in the boardinghouse, she tells her daughter what needs to be done and addresses her as "Miss Lucy California."

In the western frontier society of a California mining town of the mid-1800s, it is surprising how much the naming techniques, although not the specifics, resemble those of the medieval period. As the given names of California and her siblings show, the practice of giving place names to people was fashionable. Occupational names are seen among some of the frontiersmen, including Agamemnon Porterhouse and Poker John Lewis. The man who carries the mail across the mountains is called Snowshoe Ballou because he has such big feet. Snowshoe's only friend is an Indian named Hennit, which Snowshoe explains means "beaver" in the man's Indian language and was given to Hennit because he had thick, brown hair. Snowshoe used to have a killer duck who was so strong she was named Goliath. Snowshoe would take bets on her in the various mining camps because she was so quick and so surprising that she could beat any dog she fought—except for the last one.

Readers are not told whether Cousin Batty's name is descriptive, but they are told that Rattlesnake Jake is a villain in a story; that Jimmy Whiskers, who hangs around Lucy's mother, tells people that "curly-bearded men are industrious and make good husbands," and that the man known to the miners as the Gent shaves regularly and plays a fiddle (137).

Perhaps the most surprising similarity between the medieval stories and the western frontier story is that there were still people who, like Beetle and Runt, do not have "real" names. When Lucy is out in the woods supposedly picking berries but really reading books, she becomes friends with a runaway slave who tells her his name is Joe. He later says that *Joe* is what Mr. Sawyer called all four of the slaves he brought with him to help mine gold in California so that he didn't have to bother to remember who was who.

Lucy takes a lot longer than did Alyce in thinking up a name for her new friend. Winter is coming and she has assured him that he cannot survive in the woods and so will have to come and stay at the boarding tent. She is surprised when her mother explains that he cannot stay there, but then relents and says that perhaps they can make him a bed in the shed. When the weather forces him to accept the offer, Lucy meets him with

> "I have a present for you."
> "You ain't got no call to get me presents, missy."
> "Nevertheless, here it is." (88)

She stretches out her fist and slowly opens it. It's empty and when Joe looks puzzled, she says,

"It's a name. For you. My father's name. Bernard."

"Bernard." Joe rubbed his beard. "Bernard. It's a might fine name, missy. A name I'd be proud to carry. Bernard." (88)

Lucy stretches out her other fist and, as she opens it, tells him it's another present, another name, which is Freeman, so that his name will be Bernard Freeman. A year later when the town of Lucky Diggins has been burned to nothing but one wall and her mother's cookstove plus a few melted pots and pans, one of the men—actually the one whose building had been the source of the fire—begins accusing Bernard of bringing them bad luck. Lucy's mother comes to Bernard's rescue, and Lucy begins to rethink her friendship with Bernard, especially after her mother points out that he isn't really a man, just a boy a couple of years older than Lucy who is now fourteen.

"Must be the beard makes him look old," I said, "or his sad face." I was a little ashamed that I had never really looked at Bernard as a person but more like a plaything, something I found up by Ranger Creek, called by my father's name, and brought home to play with. (148)

She goes to Bernard and chewing on her lip tries to apologize for not realizing how young he was and for naming him like "a doll or a dog or something. You're a man—maybe you should be choosing your own name."

"I agree, missy, I agree." he answers. "And I'm choosing the name a friend offered. Bernard. I'm proud to have it." Lucy is relieved and they joke about his age. All he knows is that he has not reached twenty because Mr. Sawyer always gave twenty-year-olds a beating so "they didn't get any ideas about being grown-up and independent. And I never got that beating" (149).

Lucy tells him that it's lucky that he looks older than he is because "Mr. Sawyer will never think to look for an old man named Bernard. I guess you're pretty safe here."

"I hope you're right, Miss Lucy."

I smiled. "Just Lucy."

"I hope you're right, Just Lucy." And Bernard smiled, finally smiled. He looked much younger. (149)

Over the months, Lucy has taught Bernard to read, mostly through reading *Ivanhoe* over and over again. While Bernard is doing the cleaning up for Mr. Scatter's store he finds a newspaper from "back in the states" which tells about colored men in San Francisco who own their own businesses and help other "colored folk, even slaves." Bernard thinks he better make his way to San Francisco and get these men to help him "get free of this slavery thing" so he won't have to hide out. Cushman adds a light touch to his decision through Bernard and Lucy playing with names from their favorite book:

"So you have a heart's desire, too."
"Yes, I guess I do at that." He bowed. "Farewell, Lady Isabella."

She curtsies, slow and graceful, almost like a lady, and says:

"Godspeed, Prince Alfonso. I hope you have better luck with your heart's desire than I've had with mine." [Hers was to get back to Massachusetts.]
A week later, Bernard Freeman was gone. (158)

The saddest part of *The Ballad of Lucy Whipple* is when her brother Butte is unable to recover from his near drowning, even though "Mama fed him on slippery elm tea and onions boiled with honey, but all her tending did no good" (114). Not even Bean Belly Thompson can help when he brings from Sacramento a bottle of "Dr. Lippincott's Celebrated Lung and Nerve Tonic With Sarsaparilla, Garlic, Pennyroyal, Verbena, and Elecampane Root, Effective Against Disorders of the Lung, Hysteric Affection, and the Bite of a Mad Dog" (116).

To make the death scene bearable, Cushman adds a light touch. One of the things Butte prided himself on was collecting names for liquor while doing his job as sort of a busboy and janitor for Mr. Scatter's saloon. His goal was to collect and recite fifty such names. So far, he had only gotten to forty-eight starting with "Hooch, cactus juice, catgut, cougar's milk, gator sweat, jack-a-dandy, kingdom come, knock-me-down, mother's milk, throat tickler" and so on (70). On the night that he dies, Butte is lying "in an awful silence, no strength left even to cough. Mama, Prairie, Sierra, Brother Clyde, The Gent" and Lucy are sitting around the bed, when

> Suddenly he opened his eyes wide. "Lucy," he said, "Phlegm cutter."
> "What?"
> "Phlegm cutter. The forty-ninth word for liquor."
> He closed his eyes again. That was the last we ever heard him say. (118)

On the morning of Butte's funeral, Lucy does a lot of asking around town to find one more name for liquor. She is comforted by being able to tuck a piece of paper in his grave so that he will have reached his goal of collecting a full fifty names. It reads "Tarantula Juice."

Lucy's mother decides to marry Brother Clyde Claymore, and the family, without Lucy, goes with Brother Clyde to the Sandwich Islands (Hawaii) where he will continue his missionary work. Lucy is planning to go back East as a nanny for a well-to-do couple, but then she discovers that she has indeed become a Californian and is happy to stay in Lucky Diggins. The Green Mountain Investment Company of Poxley, Vermont, is bringing in machinery that will be able to get the gold out of the mountains. The wife of the head man, who happily explains that her entire Vermont house is being shipped in pieces to be rebuilt in Lucky Diggins, is determined to "civilize" California. Lucy is going to help, and is already in the process of creating a lending library and becoming the town librarian. Lucy writes a letter to her mother sharing all of this good news. She adds a light touch by telling how she has transplanted bulbs to Butte's grave and has also taken him one more name for liquor: *antifogmatic.* "Butte must be plumb tickled" (187). Then she ends the running battle with her mother over her name by signing the letter:

Miss California Morning Whipple,
    Happy citizen and librarian of
    Lucky Diggins, California.

It is interesting to compare this name-related ending to the name-related ending that Cushman created earlier for *Catherine, Called Birdy.* As Catherine's brother had predicted, over the course of the year that Catherine writes in her journal, she indeed "grows less childish," but who is to say whether or not it was from writing her journal? One of the marks of her new maturity is that she goes back to rethink what the old Jewish woman had said to her:

> "Remember, Little Bird, in the world to come, you will not be asked 'Why were you not George?' or 'Why were you not Perkin?' but 'Why were you not Catherine?'" And it came into my head that I cannot run away. I am who I am wherever I am. (162)

This new maturity allows her to come to terms with the idea of leaving her family home to fill the marriage vows her father has arranged. But fortunately, by now Old Shaggy Beard has been killed in a brawl over a tavern maid, and it is his son "Stephen, now Baron Selkirk, Lord of Lithgow, Smithburn, Random, and Fleece" who "wishes to honor the marriage contract in his father's place" (163). He has already sent her "an enameled brooch of a little bird with a pearl in its beak," which she is now wearing (163). In a generous mood, she releases her caged birds and confides that "mayhap Shaggy Beard was never so bad as I imagine him. Or mayhap he was," and then she prepares herself to learn to love Stephen who is

> young and clean. Loves learning, and is not Shaggy Beard. For these alone, I am prepared to love him.
> I have been making a list of names for our children. I think to call the first one George. Or Perkin. Or Edward. Or Ethelfritha. Or Magpie. Or mayhap Stephen. The world is full of possibilities.
> I leave in October. Only one month until Stephen. (164)

We will end with just a brief note about the differences and the similarities between the two time periods in names other than those given to people. The biggest difference is in the place names. The big well-established cities (e.g., Salisbury, Oxford, and London in the medieval books and San Francisco, Stockton, and Sacramento in the California book), are not particularly interesting because readers just accept them as places. More interesting are the names for small towns. Many British names for villages sound funny to modern ears because they have stayed the same way for hundreds of years while everything around them has changed. Among those mentioned in Cushman's medieval books are Wooton-Under-Wynwoode, Great Yarmouth, Gobnet-Under-Green, and Milton Abbas. These names are a far cry from the names of the small California settlements that Lucy Whipple talks about: Downieville, French Bar, Rocky Bar, Skunk Creek, Bedbug Flat, Coyote Gulch, Gravel Bar, and Ranger Creek. Most of these colorful names were short lived because as soon as developers and realtors came in they changed the names to sound pleasant enough to attract future residents or to honor successful settlers. Even Lucy daydreams with Butte about getting in the history books as "the mighty Whipples of Whippletown who struck it rich in California" (74).

In contrast, plant names, at least the ones used by common people, are fairly similar between the two periods. In *The Midwife's Apprentice*, Alyce goes to the abbey gardens to gather fallen fruit and she is overwhelmed by the different kinds of apples: "the crisp, white-fleshed Cackagees, the small, sour Foxwhelps, or the mellow, sweet Rusticoats and Rubystripes" In *Catherine, Called Birdy*, Catherine names four female puppies after the herbs Betony, Rosemary, Anise, and Rue (32), and when at the end of the book she decides to let her chamber birds fly free, she says good-bye and Godspeed to "Dittany, and Clubmoss, Wormwood, Saffron, Sage, and all the others" (159). In *The Ballad of Lucy Whipple*, Lizzie, a California girl who has "always" lived in the area, helps Lucy to see that trees are not all "just trees."

> They're oaks and firs and cedars and pines. Look here at the pines. Even they are all different. I call this one scaly pine because of the scaly look of the bark. And this one with the bark that looks like fungus I call mushroom pine. Here's smooth pine and there is mighty pine, the biggest. (124)

This is how Lucy learns the names of California plants: miner's lettuce, shooting stars, duckweed, thimbleberry, skunkbush, needlegrass, checkerbloom. She "didn't know if they were true names or Lizzie's. It didn't seem to matter" (124).

In conclusion, a look at the names in these three books by Karen Cushman shows not only how much knowledge authors need to have about the names of historical periods in which they are writing, but also about naming processes. The stories come alive not just because of the names, but because of how the characters interact both with their own names and with the names—or lack of names—of other characters in the story.

CHAPTER FOUR

~

Names to Establish Realistic Settings: Gary Soto, Adam Rapp, Meg Rosoff, and Nancy Farmer

Early in the 1990s, Gary Soto wrote that as a fairly new writer of books for young readers, he was just getting acquainted with this great body of books, and what struck him was that while the books he was reading had many literary merits, he found very little that was "obviously regional, obviously bent on nailing down a life that is wholly particular." He wrote this for the fourth edition of Donelson and Nilsen's *Literature for Today's Young Adults*[1] and lamented that he did not find mentions of real rivers or "mountains, gangs, streets, cars; in short, the particulars of the world." Place names did not matter, nor did they ring of the familiar, "such as Avocado Lake, Pinedale, Academy Cemetery, Francher's Creek, real names that might give rise to a reader's dreaming state of mind and curiosity for a faraway place." He was disappointed to find that for the most part, the books he was reading were "homogenous and widespread in their feelings and cast of characters." They lacked a sense of place and could have happened anywhere and to anyone. While such stories may be "marketable" because they do not exclude anyone, they also do not satisfy readers who know what the real world is like and want to see their world reflected in what they read.

Because Soto was first trained as a poet and "told repeatedly to go to the particular—your block, your family, your friends, some dirt pile in the backyard," he began writing about his hometown of Fresno, California, and about the particular neighborhood where he grew up, the Roosevelt High area, the industrial part of south Fresno. The neighborhood was filled with Mexican Americans, kids whose parents worked for Color Tile or the Safeway distribution center. The more he thought about it, the more he began "to see regionality and particularity as under-explored territory." He decided that there is no more reason for authors of books for teenagers than for writers for adults to try to please everyone. "We can remember the adult writers—Flannery O'Connor, Mark Twain, Sherwood Anderson, William Saroyan, Bernard Malamud—who had tenderness and longing toward place, even if that place scared the hell out of them when they were young" (82).

At the time that Soto wrote these comments, he had already published for teen readers *A Fire in My Hands: A Book of Poems* and *Baseball in April and Other Stories*, soon followed by *Local News* and *Neighborhood Odes*. *Buried Onions*, his 1997 book about a boy named Eddie who is struggling to go to City College in Fresno, is a wonderful example of a regional book. On the first page, Eddie is "sitting at a wobbly metal table on the campus of City College." As the sun climbs over the trees, he watches for the shimmering heat waves that will soon rise from the black asphalt. His theory is that these vapors are

> not released by the sun's heat but by a huge onion buried under the city. This onion made us cry. Tears leapt from our eyelashes and stained our faces. Babies in strollers pinched up their faces and wailed for no reason. Perhaps as practice for the coming years. I thought about the giant onion, that remarkable bulb of sadness. (2)

This idea of a great sadness under the Fresno valley ties the book together. When Eddie rides his bike through a new subdivision in North Fresno where the "front yards were foxholes of moist earth" waiting for shrubs and trees, he imagines that the home owners are getting ready to bury their own onions so "they could cry out their sadness right on the front lawn" (12). And at the very end of the book when Eddie is leaving the area as a new army recruit, the van has to stop for the engine to cool and Eddie wanders off into a large field that has already been harvested. He sees two men—men he had met before—who are making their living from picking up the few onions left in the field by the mechanical harvesters. Eddie, who is running away from Fresno both in sadness for the deaths and the fighting he has seen, and in fear for his own life, accepts a gift of onions from the men and "whether it was from the sun or the whipping wind, my eyes filled and then closed on the last of childhood tears" (146).

In between the first and the last allusion to onions, readers have gone with Eddie down Orange Avenue, and down First Street to the Holmes playground. They've hidden with him in an alley behind a huge cardboard box labeled "Westinghouse," and they have followed him to the army recruiting office at the Fresno Mall and to the hospital where his friend José is being treated for a gunshot wound. Eddie is glad that his friend is at least well enough to complain about the name on his hospital armband reading *Joes* instead of *José*.

One of the things that Soto's writing shows is how "place" is established not just through the names and descriptions of the neighborhoods but through a panoply of names. For example, in the first five pages of Soto's 2003 *The Afterlife*, readers get acquainted with the restroom of the Club Estrella, with *Señor GQ* (an allusion to *Gentleman's Quarterly*), with Rachel "not yet *mi novia*—my girl," with imitation Nikes and Payless shoes made of plastic, and most importantly with Jesús, who is known as Chuy at East Fresno High, but was named after his father, "whose own father was Maria Jesús, born in the 1940s in Jalisco, Mexico" (4). This kind of down-to-earth naming serves to do exactly what Gary Soto said he wanted to do, which is to provide a sense of believability and particularity to realistic stories set in his own neighborhood.

Adam Rapp's *The Buffalo Tree*

In contrast to the way that Gary Soto identifies himself as a regional writer and almost nostalgically uses names to help his readers envision or remember specific streets, parks, and neighborhoods in his hometown of Fresno, California, Adam Rapp in *The Buffalo Tree* uses both common and proper names to establish for his readers a world that he does not expect them to know. While it is not a fantasy world in the sense of science fiction or magic, for most readers it will be an imagined rather than a remembered world. The setting is a grim, tough detention center for boys under the age of sixteen. Cigarettes are referred to as squares, stretchers as body plates, payday as juvy pound, twenty dollars as two bones, wake-up call as the aurora horn, and school as study box. Stealing something is cribbing it, fighting is chucking, feeling good is having chocolate milk belly, and sneaking somewhere is using Indian feet. The boys sleep in patch holes and their bunk mates are called patch mates because the "doors" to the cells are not bars but hanging pieces of cloth. While most of the slang is not explained, early in the book Sura, the boy who is telling the story, writes:

> Coly Jo and I have been here six weeks and after blackout we take turns sleeping cause Hodge or Boo Boxfoot will creep into your room and crib shit. Hodge and Boo are on their third clip. A clip is like a year but it ain't the same. Most juvy homes don't give clips. They let you go when you make reform. But Hamstock is different. It's like Hamstock wants to keep you. (8–9)

Sura also offers an explanation of clicks, which are the sounds that the night guard makes when on his rounds he slaps his ribstick against the iron hitching post that stands in front of Spalding Cottage. The guard's ribstick is used to "bust you in the side if he catches you running for the fence" (14). At night, the boys usually get three clicks to settle down before the lights are turned out. Sura counts himself to sleep by the guard's clicks, and is upset when a new guard comes on duty and chooses not to hit the hitching post so the boys don't know where he is.

The book begins with Sura being the only white boy out of fifteen playing floor hockey "in the basement of Spalding Cottage." He imagines that if he were outside of his body and watching from the ceiling he "would look like deadness in the mass of their shiny, boiling dark, like some puppet bones" (7). But in reality, Sura is far from dead. He is small and quick with his hands. He is also the fastest runner in the institution. He fancies tucking a Newport cigarette (with a little tape on it so it will stay) behind his ear, but he never smokes because he has to keep his lungwind up for his career, which is clipping hoodies. When he steals the hood ornament from what he calls a "'77 Lincoln Clown Car" (11), the owner chases him clear across town, but Sura outruns him by cutting through a church service and jumping over the altar and out the back door. Every few days some newcomer waits for Sura outside the hash hall and challenges him to a race. They never win and Sura smugly tells himself that he has caught another rabbit.

The title of the book comes from a dead tree in front of Spalding Cottage. "If you buffalo another juvy it means you make him climb the dead tree. . . . If you're getting buffaloed you can either chuck or climb right up there and sit in those branches for everyone to see" (30). Sura suspects that most of the boys don't know the real meaning of buffalo because when he borrows Mr. Rose's pocket dictionary and looks it up he can see no relation to either the action or to the dead tree, which he wishes someone would cut down.

One of the ways that Sura and his patch mate, Coly Jo, celebrate when "they beat some juvies slinging craps" or if they "goof on some of them and get a laugh" is to "bust out" at the Telescope Pit. This is a drainage hole they discovered when they were passing the gymnasium on their way back from the hash house. It starts out big and then the ridges get smaller and smaller the further down it goes. Coly Jo and Sura piss in the hole and "cross those piss streams, too, like we're some Musketeers or something" (20).

Local allusions that allow readers to figure out that Hamstock is in Illinois include juvies getting transferred to Kankakee, which is "where they got that lucky river. If you escape, you can snatch on to some driftwood and float away" (32). When a boy turns sixteen and is too bad to be returned to regular life, he might be sent up to St. Charles, commonly called St. Chuck's. But most of the boys can look forward to the sweet-tooth clip, meaning they will get released on their "Sweet Sixteenth birthday" (50).

If Rapp wanted readers to feel familiar with the world he was writing about, he could have portrayed Sura as being proud of his Nike or his L. L. Bean windbreaker, but instead Sura is proud of his Red Troutman's fireproof windbreaker, especially after he leaves it hanging on a chair so the wrinkles fall out (11). Sura's patch mate Coly Jo's prized possession was a Barnum Fletcher squirrel-skin cap, which got cribbed the first two days he was there. Now Boo (the biggest bully) wears it around "like it's something his moms sent him" (9). Sura refers to his "moms" as Mazzy and her new boyfriend as Flintlock. He calls attractive girls Choate Street honeys, the kitchen help old hash-house honeys, and the janitor Mop Man. Mr. Rose is their cottage pops, while the disciplinarian, who has a two-foot paddle made out of body-box wood, is Dean Petty. Dean is probably his given name, not a title. When one of the boys has escaped and a visitor comes carrying a metal clipboard and asking lots of questions, Dean Petty turns into Dean Smoothy. Sura quibbles with the two men over whether they are talking about "Mister Sheridan" or about the boy everyone calls "Long Neck." Sura is offended that a man who doesn't even know him is there "talking with his eyes" to Dean Smoothy and hinting that they could probably lighten Sura's clip a bit if he would tell them what he knows (167).

Sura calls the counselor, who is his official "path mentor," Deacon Bob Fly. He plays mental games when Fly shows him what Sura calls "splot cards," and early on he displays his disdain for the man by surmising that he probably drives "one of those non-smooth American rides," something like a gray Ford Fairmont or an Olds that doesn't even have a hoody. Even worse, it probably has an AM radio and a pleather interior. "There ain't nothing sadder than a pleather interior" (35).

Hostilities among the boys are intense. When they wait in line for food, they have to stand face-to-the-back-of-the-head so there is no eye contact. But that doesn't keep them from talking as soon as the guards have passed them by. A "game" that Sura hates is when the bullies start making fun of and threatening someone named Ock. "The thing about 'Ock' is that you never know who he is. Sometimes you think 'Ock' could be one juvy, and sometimes you think 'Ock' could be eleven juvies" (95). Sura looks up the meanings of words he doesn't know, like one time he looked up *Mastiff* and found a picture of a St. Bernard and could see why Mastiff was a good nickname for the boy who had it, but he can't find *Ock* and concludes that it is one of those nonwords that the bullies use to keep the other kids guessing.

Another name that the bully named Hodge uses is Sham. When he is close enough to kids that they can hear him, he talks to himself saying things like "Got me another one, Sham. Got me another one" (32). A newcomer thought it was cool and called Hodge "Sham." Hodge does not forgive his mistake and drives the point home by waiting until the boy is asleep and then setting his hair on fire.

A cursory description of the plot and setting that Adam Rapp devised for *The Buffalo Tree* is similar to what Louis Sachar devised for the contemporary part of *Holes*, but when it comes to tone, the books are far apart. One difference is that in *Holes*, the really "bad stuff" happened long ago so it isn't as frightening. Also, at Camp Green Lake the hostility is softened with humor and there is a sense of comradeship among the boys as they unite against Mr. Sir, Mr. Pedanski, and the warden. In contrast, most of the boys in Rapp's book are vicious to each other, while the adults are reprehensible. This means that readers are likely to remember *The Buffalo Tree* as tragic, while they remember *Holes* as comic. Both authors make extensive use of character and place names, but the fact that the results are so different illustrates the kind of control that skilled authors can exert over both their techniques and their content.

Meg Rosoff's *How I Live Now:* A Novel

In simplified terms, Rosoff's novel, which won the 2005 Printz Award, is the story of seven years in the life of Daisy, whose father originally named her Elizabeth, but was mistaken because, according to Daisy, she never "had the face of someone dignified and sad like an old-fashioned queen or a dead person" (1). At the beginning of the book, which Daisy narrates, she is a fifteen-year-old New York anorexic who is being sent to live with cousins on a farm in England. Her mother died giving birth to her, and her father has fairly recently remarried. Daisy calls her father's new wife Davina the Diabolical or D the D (11). This stepmother, who Daisy says did not "make even the slightest attempt to address centuries of bad press for stepmothers," is expecting a baby. Daisy and her friend, Leah, vow to call it Damian "even if it's a girl" (11).

Daisy says her food problem started when she was afraid that D the D wanted to poison her, but then she confesses that it becomes very satisfying to have both parents worrying about her. The decision to send her to live somewhere else is apparently a last-ditch effort. She travels thousands of miles and is surprised to be met at the airport by a fourteen-year-old boy named Edmond, who smokes and drives the family's jeep across medians and up do-not-enter ramps to avoid paying the airport's parking fee. He can also read Daisy's mind, but she doesn't find this out until later. On the long drive to the family's farm, which is more like an estate in grand old movies than a typical American farm,

Daisy falls asleep. When they arrive, she is warmly greeted by Edmond's seventeen-year-old twin brothers, Osbert and Isaac, his nine-year-old sister, Piper, and the black and white dogs, Jet and Gin, along with assorted cats and a goat named Dink. There's no sign of her mother's sister, Aunt Penn, and Daisy begins to wonder if maybe she has died and no one knows quite how to break the news.

But after a long nap, Daisy meets Aunt Penn, who apologizes and explains that she has to "give a lecture in Oslo . . . on the Imminent Threat of War," and because she has work to do she needs to be excused (15). She assures Daisy that she will be gone only a few days and the children will take good care of her. Daisy thinks, "There's that old war again, popping up like a bad penny. . . . Would There Be One or Wouldn't There" (15). In fact, war does break out and Aunt Penn is eventually killed trying to get back home, but it is several months before the children learn about her death. The part of the story that gets a large share of attention from reviewers and readers is that Daisy and her cousin Edmond become lovers. We are writing relatively little about that because Rosoff does not rely on literary uses of names to tell the unusual love story.

Early on, Rosoff uses a variety of names to introduce readers to Daisy's quirky sense of humor as well as to remind them that Daisy is an American in a strange land—as when she compares "the concrete jungle" of the Upper West Side of New York to "Walt Disney on Ecstasy" (53), which is how she describes spring on the farm. She wonders why "Ye-olde English version of a 7-Eleven" (26) is also a post office and a drugstore, and when she and Piper are moved to live with a family, she bemoans having to work so hard to keep her "fake smile" from resembling that of Jason in *Friday the 13th* (74). Later, when she and Piper are trying to survive as they make their way back to the family's house, she is grateful for Piper's knowledge of nature because she wouldn't have recognized an edible nut if it tapped her on the shoulder and asked for the way "to Carnegie Hall" (124).

Daisy remembers a painting that she once had to copy in art class called *The Calm before the Storm*. It was totally peaceful except for a greenish black part "up in one corner which was obviously The Storm" (29). The name keeps jumping into Daisy's mind as she notes the growing tensions when a couple from London comes down to stay in their "weekend house . . . for The Duration." They have two children and a "purebred Bouvier des Flandres, which turns out to be a dog" (42). As they confidently tell everyone, they think they will be "a whole lot safer" here than in London; Daisy is not so sure because "the locals" are suddenly getting all "Them and Us." Even though they treat the couple with a fair amount of courtesy, Daisy thinks that under the surface, they hate this pretentious couple and are just waiting to get even when the food runs out.

An interesting technique that Rosoff uses throughout the book is to capitalize key words and phrases. The effect is almost as if she is turning these phrases into names, and because she avoids using quotation marks the capitalization carries extra weight as when Daisy states that her mother died in childbirth and complains about not being told more about her mother than that "Good Old Mom" died to give her life. Daisy's dad is a "Never Mention Her Name Again type" (19), and she suspects that she would have had a happier life without the label of "Murderer" or "Poor Motherless Lamb" (19).

When Rosoff writes about the war, this kind of capitalization enables her to communicate a great deal about the war without ever naming the enemy. She talks about Bad Guys and Good Guys and about a visitor she calls Mr. Regular Army and his Man Friday. By not naming the enemy, Rosoff plays with readers' emotions by encouraging them to fill in the blanks with the name of whatever or whomever they fear the most.

At the beginning of the war, the children enjoy being on their own. Then, a couple of bored men come "From the Council" to register them and "Determine their Medical and Nutritional Exigencies" (38), which is little more than seeing if they have appendicitis or scurvy. Rosoff uses the following phrases capitalized as shown to drop hints about the war: "London . . . Occupied . . . Really Going On . . . Malign Forces . . . The Wireless . . . More Recent Information . . . weren't At Liberty" (40). On the next page, Daisy presents a sample of the things people say while waiting in line for their food rations.

1. My brother-in-law says it's the French bastards.
2. My friend in Chelsea said the looting is terrible and she got the most amazing wide-screen TV.

3. My neighbor in The Lords says it's the Chinese.
4. Have you noticed no Jews have been killed?
5. There's a nuclear bunker under Marks & Spencer that's only open to shareholders.
6. People are eating their pets
7. The Queen is Bearing Up.
8. The Queen is Breaking Down.
9. The Queen is one of Them. (41)

Pretty soon there is an "alleged" smallpox epidemic, and the authorities send out notices saying that people are no longer to be out on the streets; their food will be delivered. Whispers abound as to where the food is coming from: The Red Cross? The Americans? The Enemy? Just in case it is the latter, some people refuse to touch it.

In the few letters that Daisy gets from home, her father tells her to be careful "not to become a Victim of the Terrorist Threat" (32). A letter from her friend Leah is more entertaining. She "reports that Ms. Cool Herself, Melissa Banner, was going around telling everyone that she and Lyle Hershberg were Hooking up" (32). Daisy does not believe this because Melissa is the world's "most famous living professional virgin," and Lyle told his last girlfriend "that if she didn't Satisfy His Needs at least three times a day he'd have to find relief elsewhere" (33). Daisy's friend, Leah, had walked in on Lyle "Satisfying His Needs all by himself in homeroom" and said to him, "Well well well Lyle Hershberg, don't look now but there's a Smurf with a hard-on in your pants" (33). Daisy doubts that Leah could have thought that fast; nevertheless several weeks later when she and Piper are sent to live with a family and are given the older boy's bedroom, Daisy looks at the posters of racing cars and "some teeny-bop star with cellulite" and decides that the room has "seen a fair amount of action à la Lyle Hershberg and his pet Smurf" (75).

The occupation eventually ends, but not before all five of the family have witnessed terrible things. Daisy and Piper are the first to make it back home, and after a couple of days are shocked when the telephone rings and it is Daisy's father. He immediately goes into high gear to get his daughter "evacuated" from the war zone. Back in the States, Daisy is first hospitalized, and then institutionalized, and finally released "to wait." As she explains, she took a job and read books and filled out forms and spent time in air raid shelters. Basically she "stayed alive," but nothing distracted her from waiting. "The. Time. Simply. Passed" (170).

It is six years before she can make her way back to her cousins and to Edmond, who has lived in almost a catatonic state. She learns that he arrived home only two days after her "evacuation." He was already traumatized by having seen the massacre at the neighboring farm and was all the more damaged to find Daisy gone. Piper says that he did not speak for a year, and the only thing that seemed to help him was gardening, something that he still does. But what Daisy sees in the tangle of the garden isn't "beauty. Passion, maybe. And something else. Rage" (181).

Edmond at first shows no sign of recognizing Daisy, but as the days go by and she becomes a gardener "of sorts," the two of them gradually begin to reconnect. On the next to the last page, Rosoff uses the scientific names of plants as a way to reveal their new relationship. When they go for walks, Edmund tells her the names of the plants they see. Daisy worries that there are too many of them, and the only ones she manages to keep in her head are the ones that kept her and Piper alive when they were scavenging for food. The simplicity, and at the same time the complexity, of the paragraph reveals the challenge that lies ahead for Daisy and Edmond:

Corylus avellana. Hazelnuts. Rubus fruticosus. Blackberries. Agaricus campestris. Field mushrooms. Rorippa nasturtium-aquaticum. Watercress. Allium ursinum. Wild garlic. Malus domestica. Apples. (193)

Nancy Farmer's A Girl Named Disaster

Nancy Farmer in A Girl Named Disaster is so eager to inform readers about life in present-day Mozambique and Zimbabwe, where she lived for many years while her husband worked as a water purification specialist, that she fills her book with hundreds of authentic names and details. The book was a 1996 National Book Award finalist and a 1997 Newbery Honor Book. In an afterword, Farmer explains that the story takes place in 1981 when there was considerable hostility among white people, the Shona, and the Matebele (299), and crossing borders was dangerous because of the many land mines planted along the way. The

book is divided into three parts. The first is set in a traditional Moza-
mique village, the second is a yearlong journey (mostly by water), and
the third is in Zimbabwe at the Efifi scientific research station and seventy miles south in or near the Zimbabwe city of Mtoroshanga.

The heroine is Nhamo, an eleven-year-old orphan who lives with
her deceased mother's extended family in a remote village near the
Mkumbura River, which feeds into the huge man-made Lake Cabora
Bassa. Nhamo is a modern-day Cinderella, loved only by her grandmother, her *Ambuya*. Even though at birth she was given a name that
translates into "disaster," the real disaster of her life occurs when she is
three years old. On a bright, sunny afternoon, she and her mother are
asleep in their hut when a leopard comes in and walks right past the
sleeping child and kills the mother. "Nhamo couldn't remember the
tragedy, yet somewhere inside her was a memory of flowing, spotted
skin and terrible claws" (6). And because Nhamo has heard the story
so many times, leopards are the one thing she is deathly afraid of.

It is not until page 51 that readers learn why Nhamo was given her
name. Her family has gone for a rare visit to town and as Ambuya gets
a little tipsy from the beer that the Portuguese owner of the trading post
gives her, she entertains the loafers (the *tsotsis*) sitting on the front
porch with an explanation of why Nhamo, her "wonderful Little Pumpkin" and the only child of her beautiful daughter Runako, was given
such a name. Runako was so smart she even had a scholarship (a *bon-
sella*) to attend the Catholic school, but then one day she comes home
with a bulging stomach, followed by a man who was a "scheming
hyena! Not a coin in his pockets, not a cow to his name" (53). This
man, named *Proud* Jongwe, is Nhamo's father. He is from Zimbabwe
and all he does is drink and fight. One night in a bar before Nhamo is
born, he kills a man named Goré Mtoko, who during a fight had pushed
Proud into a bed of hot coals. Proud runs away to return to his family
and work in the Mtoroshanga chrome mines.

Nhamo is horrified at learning—especially in front of a group of
strangers—that no *roora* (bride-price) had been paid for her mother;
she was "worthless." When the other family members come to fetch
Ambuya and Nhamo from the trading post, Aunt Chipo observes dis-
approvingly that Ambuya has been drinking, and Uncle Kufa says quietly, "I thought we agreed never to talk about Runako's husband." Am-

buya answers belligerently, "Am I to fill my mouth with clay? Am I to be lectured by one who was wetting his loincloth when I was out buying cattle for my family?" (54).

As Nhamo thinks about her grandmother telling the story on the porch of the trading post, she realizes that Ambuya is not a typical woman of her tribe; she maintains a level of independence and control quite unlike that of other women. Because she has money and paid the family of the man who was killed by Nhamo's father, she sees no reason to keep the sad affair secret. Ambuya's strength stands Nhamo in good stead when a short while later, the village decides that the epidemic of cholera that is killing both old and young is caused by the leopard spirit of the man killed by Nhamo's father. The only way to assuage him is for Nhamo to marry the man's older brother. The man has a bad reputation and three much older wives, who everyone knows will resent Nhamo and make her life even worse than it is now.

While these decisions are being made, Ambuya suffers a stroke, but she nevertheless calls Nhamo into her room and tells her she must flee. Ambuya has figured out that Nhamo may be Catholic since her parents were married as Catholics, and so she can go and seek help from the nuns and maybe find her father. "He's as trustworthy as a rat in a grain bin, but he's all you've got" (80). She tells Nhamo to take the boat that had belonged to the recently deceased fisherman Crocodile Guts and because of the land mines, not to get out of the boat until she is well into Zimbabwe. She is to follow the village river until it comes to the Musengezi, and then she must use the paddle to force the boat *against* the flow.

She instructs Nhamo about the supplies she needs to gather, and then she has Nhamo close the door for privacy. Ambuya gives Nhamo her life savings of gold nuggets that she has gathered from the stream. She tells Nhamo to put them in a bag and tie them around her neck, and not to trade them or sell them without getting advice from the nuns. She will know that she is in Zimbabwe when she sees electric lights "bright as a hundred fires" (79).

That evening, Nhamo sets out on a journey that should take only a few days, but instead takes almost a year because Nhamo misses the point where she is to row the boat against the current and ends up lost in the huge Lake Cabora Bassa that was formed as a result of dams being built. She lives for a while on an island uninhabited except for animals, mostly baboons, but also a leopard, which frightens her. At last she realizes that she does not want to grow old and die all alone. And so with the kind of strength that would make Ambuya proud, she builds herself a new boat and sails toward what she hopes will be Zimbabwe.

She eventually makes it to Zimbabwe and, because of her fear of land mines, follows an elephant's tracks through a forest. It leads her to the Efifi research center where she is picked up by one of the women scientists and taken into the center's clinic, a small hospital. She is referred to as the Wild Child and is treated for malaria, bilharzia, and malnutrition. There are no other children around Efifi because the workers go home to their own houses at night, and the research lab is not considered a healthy place for children. As Nhamo gets better, she begins to help take care of the animals and to do various tasks. She tells her story in bits and pieces, and at last she is taken seventy miles south for a fairly long visit with her father's family.

The first thing that Nhamo learns at the Jongwes is that her father is dead, but her uncle's family gives her a welcome of sorts and lets her stay long enough for her to decide that she does not want the kind of life they have. Fortunately, the great-grandfather is still alive. His name is Murenga Jongwe, but he is mostly called the *nganga*, a title reserved for the head of a family. He confides to Nhamo that both he and she are embarrassments to the family because the family wants to be modern, and the two of them are reminders of the old days. He tells Nhamo how his son, Jongwe Senior, dug a tunnel into one of the mountains in the Umvukwe Range, which is now like a giant anthill because so many people have dug into it. Jongwe Senior was lucky and found chrome.

> As soon as he got money, he began to imitate the white people, and he changed his Shona name, Murenga, to Lloyd. He wanted to flatter the owner of the Big Chief Chrome Company, who was also called Lloyd. Unfortunately, the owner was killed by a land mine. Then the whites began to lose the war and it became unfashionable to have a white name. . . . As you know, the word *murenga* means "revolution." What wonderful luck! Lloyd-the-lackey turned into Murenga-the-revolutionary overnight. (281)

Great-Grandfather tells this to Nhamo on the day he takes her up to the mines to show her where her father had dug his own tunnel in hopes of getting rich, but was killed when the mountain caved in. His body was never recovered. The nganga goes on to say that his son, Murenga-the-revolutionary, was first in line for the victory parades and that he himself was "promoted from being a senile old peasant to being a revered elder" (282). Murenga named his two sons Proud and Industry. They must have been born during the phase when Murenga was trying to imitate white men, which is why he gave them English words for names. Or maybe this is still the fashion, because he recently took a second wife and is father to a young boy who is named Clever.

As Nhamo has observed in her visit to the family, Murenga is an alcoholic, and her Great-Grandfather explains that "Proud was a good boy. . . . He could have been such a fine man, but he started drinking when he was no older than you. I think he used to empty Murenga's bottles after he passed out" (282). When Proud fell in love with the beautiful schoolgirl who became Nhamo's mother, Murengo did not want him to marry, but the nganga approved and the couple was married by the Catholic priest, who made sure that they got an official license. Nhamo is relieved to know that at least her parents were married, even if her father never paid the bride-price. When they get home, Great-Grandfather gives Nhamo her parents' wedding portrait and promises to also give her their marriage certificate so that Nhamo will have proof that she is a Jongwe, even though the nganga is no longer sure this is such a good thing.

Nhamo's fear of leopards connects to an important name-related part of the plot based on the Shona custom of giving children the father's totem name, which identifies their clan. In the back of the book, Farmer explains that totem names are taken from animals or parts of animals. People are forbidden to eat the animal of their totem name and are also forbidden to marry someone with the same totem name. People also have *chidao* or "praise names," but the totem names are the most important. When Nhamo's great-grandfather, the nganga, takes her up the mountain to see where her father was killed and to tell her the family history, he explains that when two powerful clans are joined family members sometimes keep the totem names from both families. Nhamo thinks that the totem name for the Jongwes is Lion, but the nganga tells Nhamo that actually their family totem is more Leopard than Lion. Her father, Proud, chose to use the Lion part of their name because he thought it seemed more powerful, but in reality Proud "was really more like a leopard. A leopard hunts alone in the shadows. He doesn't face his enemies openly" (284).

The man that Proud had killed in their village belonged to the same clan as the Jongwes. When the nganga says, "Goré Mtoko's totem was the leopard. So is ours," Nhamo is appalled because "if two people with the same totem married, it was *incest*" (284). When the nganga sees her horrified reaction, he hastens to explain that the Mtokos are very distant relatives. Her marriage to Goré Mtoko's older brother would "not have been incest, although it would certainly have been evil" (284). Then he goes on to give his interpretation of Nhamo's relationship to leopards and leopard spirits.

First, he tells her that Goré Mtoko's leopard spirit was probably what killed her mother and also what caused the mountain to collapse and kill her father, but her later dealings with leopards were more likely to have come from her father's unsatisfied leopard spirit. Very early in the story, Nhamo is coming home late from gathering firewood, and is frightened when she has to cross the river near the banana grove. When she is scolded for being late, she says that she was kept away by a leopard. In the back of her mind, she suspects it was her imagination as the dusky light played tricks with shadows, but still she tells everyone about it, and the nganga believes that this is the first time she was visited by her father's leopard spirit. During the cholera epidemic, there are rumors of leopards being in the same banana grove and of leopard tracks being seen on new graves. This is how the villagers developed the idea that the epidemic was being caused by the leopard spirit of the murdered Goré Mtoko.

The nganga's interpretation is that all of this was a good thing, not the disaster that Nhamo thinks it is. He says that Proud's leopard spirit was at work to drive Nhamo away from her mother's village and toward his family. When Nhamo asks,

"But the leopard on the island—"
"Tell me, did it ever harm you?"
"No," Nhamo admitted.
"From what you told me, it provided you with meat when you most needed it, and killed the baboon that was a danger to you. At the same

time, it frightened you off the island. Otherwise you might have spent the rest of your life there."
Nhamo clasped her hands. That was certainly true.
"Proud appeared to me in a dream recently, asking me to bring you here. I think he wanted you to understand what he had done." (284–85)

Even in relating this small part of the story, it was a challenge for us to keep the character names straight and to know which ones were translations and which were English names given by Shona speakers. Farmer undoubtedly faced a challenge in deciding how to balance her desire to use "authentic" versus "translated" names while writing a complicated, three-hundred-page book that would appeal to young readers. Probably as a help to herself as a writer, as well as a help to her readers, at the front of the book she provides three maps showing increasingly detailed drawings of the setting and the placement of Nhamo's village and the huge lake. She also provides a "Cast of Characters" in five groupings: "The Village," "The Trading Post," "The Journey," "Efifi," and "Mtoroshanga" (the home of the Jongwes). "The Journey" characters include the generic name for water spirits (the *Njuzu*) and a witch named Long Teats, as well as the baboons that become Nhamo's companions on the island. Apparently, Farmer decided to simplify matters by translating into English the names given to animals, as when she has Nhamo call the baboons that shared the island with her Rumpy, Fat Cheeks, Donkeyberry, and Tag. In an earlier story that Nhamo told, she included two dogs with the names of Bit Hard and Grip Fast. Also the name of such background characters as Crocodile Guts and Long Teats are apparently translations, while the names listed for the Efifi research station are in English because that is how the people are known: Dr. Hendrik van Heerden; Dr. Everjoice Masuku; Sister Gladys, a nurse; and *Baba* Joseph, a Vapostori Christian, who cares for the animals and especially appreciates Nhamo's help.
At the end of the book, Farmer provides a glossary giving definitions for ninety-three non-English words. Of these, nineteen are the names of plants while eight are the names of tools or instruments unique to the area. With either of these sets, as well as with interjections and swear words and the names of political groups, religious terms, and clan names, translations would have been awkward. However, Farmer also

includes the native words for ten familial titles such as *mother, aunt, grandmother, father,* and so on, and for twenty common nouns including such words as *mealie* for "corn," *meisie-kind* for "girl" or "child," and *tsotsi* for "hoodlum." Since these words could have been translated fairly easily, Farmer must have chosen to use the Shona words for literary purposes, probably to keep reminding her readers that the story is set in a culture very different from their own.

As pleased as we are to find a book that makes such heavy use of authentic names and naming customs, we suspect that the continuing popularity of the book will be based on the willingness of those who have read it to bring it to the attention of other capable and committed readers. Students looking for a thin book for a weekend assignment are going to be discouraged when thumbing through the three hundred pages of *A Girl Named Disaster* and seeing two or three italicized and hard-to-pronounce names per page, along with occasional footnotes, plus fifteen pages of "extra" explanations and suggested further readings at the back. Nevertheless, we predict that *A Girl Named Disaster* will become what Farmer describes as a "stealth" best seller, which year after year attracts a substantial number of readers who keep the book in print by recommending it to other readers. *A Girl Named Disaster* is the happy result of a talented writer having both the experience and the knowledge to write a coming-of-age story that demonstrates both the universality and the uniqueness of naming practices in a culture very different from that of its readers.

Note

1. Gary Soto, "On the Particulars of the World," in *Literature for Today's Young Adults,* 4th edition, by Alleen Pace Nilsen and Kenneth L. Donelson. New York: Harper Collins, 1993, 82.

~

CHAPTER FIVE

Names to Establish Imagined Settings: Yann Martel, Orson Scott Card, and Ursula K. Le Guin

Folklorists who study urban legends say that one of the main reasons these stories are believed by so many people is that they are filled with concrete details, including names that lull listeners into suspending their disbelief. For example, here in Arizona the story of the set of free tickets sent to families to get them out of the way while their house is robbed is always said to be to a Phoenix Suns basketball game, while the early legend about a woman shopper having her purse plucked from the hook on a restroom door was always said to have happened in Goldwater's, the upscale department store now taken over by a chain but originally owned by Barry Goldwater's family.

Such local touches provide grounding that gives people confidence in believing the rest of the story. This is why many authors of fantasy and science fiction start their books by using names with real-life connections. Once they have pulled readers into trusting them, then they begin to create and use the unique names that fit only in the worlds of their imagination.

Yann Martel's prizewinning *Life of Pi* provides a good example of an author creating a fantasy story, but starting it so realistically that readers have a hard time telling exactly when they realize the book isn't true. *Life of Pi* was chosen as the 2004 One-Book-for-Arizona and when Martel came to Phoenix in April of 2004 to participate in a celebration panel he said that one of his goals was to lead readers so carefully into the fantasy elements of the story that they will get his messages (mainly about ecology and religion) before they realize that they are reading a fantasy rather than a survival-at-sea story.

The story begins in Pondicherry, India, when sixteen-year-old Pi Patel is getting ready to migrate to Canada with his family. The Patel family's move is more complicated than most because Pi's father manages the Pondicherry Zoo, which is closing. Several of the largest and most exotic animals are going with the family to be placed in American zoos, while the family makes its new life in Winnipeg, Canada. Both the family and the animals will be traveling on the *Tsimtsum*, a Panamanian-registered Japanese cargo ship with Japanese officers and a Taiwanese crew. The ship sinks, and Pi, along with a few of the zoo animals, is apparently the only survivor. The story of his months at sea make up the main part of the book, but before the sinking of the ship, Martel has made sure that readers know and love his main character.

On page 8, Pi launches forth with an explanation: "I was named after a French swimming pool. Quite peculiar considering my parents never took to water" (8). The person who suggested the name is Francis Adirubasamy, who is such a good friend of the family that Pi grew up calling him *Mamaji* (*mama* is the Tamil word for "uncle," while—*ji* is a suffix indicating respect and affection). As a young man, Mamaji was an Olympic swimmer and the champion of all south India. He never tires of telling the Patel family about the great pools he has swum in, especially the Piscine Molitor, which he describes as the "crowning glory of Paris" and maybe "the entire civilized world" (11). Since Mamaji believes that even the gods would have wanted to swim in it, he convinces the Patels that they should name their younger son, born three years after Ravi, Piscine Molitor Patel.

At school, Pi has trouble with his strange name. Some people think that he is an Indian Sikh by the name of *P. Singh*. Pi's classmates call him *Pissing Patel*, and ask "Where's Pissing? I've got to go," or they say, "You're facing the wall. Are you Pissing?" After these taunts, "the sound would disappear, but the hurt would linger, like the smell of piss long after it has evaporated" (20). On hot days when geography lessons stretched out like the Thar Desert and history lessons became parched and dusty, even the teachers would forget "the fresh aquatic promise of my name" and would call on me with "Yes, Pissing" (21). When Pi reaches "the swimming age," which Mamaji insists is seven, he takes Pi down to the beach, spreads his arms seaward, and says, "This is my gift to you" (9). From then on, three times a week he takes Pi, who is the only one in the family at all interested, for swimming lessons, something which later saves his life. What saves Pi's emotional life is an idea he inaugurates on his first day at Petit Séminaire (high school). When it comes time for each student to announce his name, Piscine goes to the chalkboard and writes:

MY NAME IS
PISCINE MOLITOR PATEL,
KNOWN TO ALL AS
PI PATEL

For good measure, he also draws the Pi symbol equaling 3.14 and makes a large circle sliced in two "with a diameter to evoke the basic lesson of geometry." He repeats the stunt in each class: "Repetition is important in the training not only of animals but also of humans" and miraculously it works (23). His older brother teases him, but just a little, for being so fond of yellow that he changes his name to Lemon Pie.

By filling the story with unusual names, Martel pulls readers into the life of Pi's family while getting them accustomed to the idea of an exotic setting. On June 21, 1977, when the family goes to the dock to board the *Tsimtsum*, Pi's mother is dressed in her most beautiful sari. She is sad to be leaving "India of the heat and monsoons, of rice fields and the Cauvery River, of friends and known shopkeepers, of Nehru Street and Boubert Salis, of this and that, India so familiar to her and loved by her." She points to a cigarette wallah and asks, "Should we get a pack or two?"

Her husband, who like Pi and his older brother, Ravi, is "a Winnipegger at heart already," responds with "They have tobacco in Canada, and why do you want to buy cigarettes? We don't smoke" (90). As Pi ponders on why his mother is even thinking of buying cigarettes, he decides that she is not worried about getting the basics of life in Canada, but she is worried about missing all the things she associates with home. She quite rightly suspects that the packaging and the brand names will be different. The cigarettes will not be Gold Flake, nor will the ice cream be Arun, or the bicycles Heroes, or the televisions Onidas. The family will miss seeing Ambassador cars and Higginbotham bookshops, and so at the last minute Pi's mother is looking for some little bit of India small enough she can tuck it in her purse.

Much later after the disaster when Pi has been at sea for months, he begins to worry that he will run out of survival rations and reduces his intake of food to only two biscuits every eight hours. This leaves him in constant hunger, and he begins to dream and obsess about food. He wants a meal the size of India, soup flowing like the Ganges, and ice cream piled as high as the Himalayas. In his mind he sees "Hot chappatis the size of Rajasthan, Bowls of rice as big as Uttar Pradesh" and "Sambars to flood all of Tamil Nadu" (212).

These exotic names serve to make the one "normal" name in the story stand out as different and therefore worthy of attention. Readers meet the owner of the ordinary name at the beginning of part 2, entitled "Pacific Ocean." In the middle of the night on its fourth day out from Manila, "midway to Midway" (101) the *Tsimtsum*, which had been moving "with the slow, massive confidence of a continent" sinks with a sound "like a monstrous metallic burp" (100). Pi, who has heard a sound and gotten up in the night to investigate, finds himself alone in a lifeboat, but then he sees something in the water and shouts out:

> Jesus, Mary, Muhammad and Vishnu, how good to see you, Richard Parker! Don't give up, please. Come to the lifeboat. Do you hear this whistle? TREEEEEEE! TREEEEEEE! TREEEEEEE! You heard right. Swim, swim! You're a strong swimmer. It's not a hundred feet. (97)

Suddenly Pi realizes what he is doing, and changes his tone, because Richard Parker is a four-hundred-pound Bengal tiger. So he screams, "Let go of that lifebuoy, Richard Parker. Let go, I said. I don't want you here, do you understand? Go somewhere else. Leave me alone. Get lost. Drown! Drown!" (99).

However, by now the tiger is pulling himself onto the boat, and so begins the real survival story. Richard Parker was named as the result of a clerical error. A panther had been terrorizing the Khulna district of

Bangladesh. Among those searching for him was a hunter named Richard Parker. He came upon a tiger and its cub, which he took to the train station for delivery to the Pondicherry Zoo. The shipping clerk was so befuddled by all the commotion that he mistakenly fills in the blanks to show that the tiger cub's name was Richard Parker, the hunter's first name was Thirsty, and his family name was None Given.

Shortly after Richard Parker comes aboard, Pi sees another animal floating toward him "on an island of bananas in a halo of light, as lovely as the Virgin Mary. The rising sun was behind her. Her flaming hair looked stunning." He shouts out, "Oh blessed Great Mother, Pondicherry fertility goddess, provider of milk and love, wondrous arm spread of comfort, terror of ticks, picker-up of crying ones, are you to witness this tragedy too?" He is greeting Orange-Juice "so called because she tended to drool" and also because she was the "prize Borneo orang-utan matriarch, zoo star and mother of two fine boys" (111).

Pi loves animals and has fun with them and their names. After a rainstorm has left water in the bottom of the part of the boat he has assigned to the tiger, he cautiously dips his beaker into what he calls Parker's Pond. And when he decides that the only way he can survive on his strange Noah's Ark is to train Richard Parker as though he were a circus animal, he goes through the patter of a barker welcoming his imaginary audience "TO THE GREATEST SHOW ON EARTH." He renames his lifeboat "THE PI PATEL, INDO-CANADIAN, TRANS-PACIFIC, FLOATING CIRCUUUUUSSSSSSSSSS!!!" (165).

When he passes through a group of whales "a short-lived archipelago of volcanic islands," he is convinced that they understand his condition and he imagines their conversation:

> Oh! It's that castaway with the pussy cat; *Bamphoo* was telling me about. Poor boy. Hope he has enough plankton. I must tell *Mumphoo* and *Tomphoo* and *Stimphoo* about him. I wonder if there isn't a ship around I could alert. His mother would be very happy to see him again. Goodbye, my boy. I'll try to help. My name's *Pimphoo*. And so through the grapevine, every whale of the Pacific knew of me. (230)

Years later, when Pi is a grown man living in Canada, he relates a couple of incidents about names that remind the reader that even though Pi is no longer in India he is still struggling to find his identity and to promote his multicultural ideas about religion. In the first incident, he orders a pizza and is so frustrated at trying to explain his name over the telephone, that he says, "I am who I am." The pizza comes delivered to Ian Houlihan. In the second incident, he tells how for many years his foster mother, a Québécoise, thinks that Hare Krishnas are "Hairless Christians." When he corrects her, he tells her that she has made a true observation in that underneath the outside trappings religions are not as different from each other as people think. The kindness and love that Hindus feel make them "indeed hairless Christians," while Muslims, "in the way they see God in everything, are bearded Hindus," and Christians have a kind of devotion that makes them "hat-wearing Muslims" (50).

Part 3 of the book, the denouement, takes only thirty pages to present an alternate version of Pi's story. It is entitled "Benito Juárez Infirmary, Tomatlán, Mexico," and begins with a place-name story. Mr. Tomohiro Okamoto and his junior colleague, Mr. Atsuro Chiba, from the Maritime Department in the Japanese Ministry of Transport are in Long Beach, California, when they hear that a lone survivor of the Japanese ship *Tsimtsum*, which mysteriously disappeared several months earlier, has landed near the small town of Tomatlán and is now recovering in the town's infirmary. Mr. Okamoto and Mr. Chiba are instructed to go and interview this survivor to see what they can learn about the sinking of their ship. They buy a map of Mexico to see where Tomatlán is, but unfortunately Mr. Okamoto makes an error when he reads the folded map. He mistakes a small coastal town named Tomatán for Tomatlán (289). Because this town is just halfway down Baja, California, the two men decide to drive. When they get there and discover their mistake, they decide to drive two hundred more kilometers further south and take a ferry across the Gulf of California to Guaymas, from where they have to drive as far south as Mexico City. They have a flat tire and then their rented car breaks down. A dishonest mechanic cannibalizes the motor of their car by trading used parts for their new ones, which of course causes further breakdowns and overcharges by a new mechanic. By the time Mr. Okamoto and Mr. Chiba arrive at Pi's bedside, they have endured forty-one hours of nonstop traveling and are very tired and almost—but not quite—ready to believe whatever story Pi chooses to tell them about the sinking of the ship and how he has survived long enough to arrive at Tomatlán. Pi tells them the story that readers have just been privy to. When they look unsatisfied, he gives them the shorter, more believable account. They still look unsatisfied, and so Pi presses them to say which is the "best story." They admit that the longer version, the one with the animals in it, is the "best story," but they nevertheless shake their heads and go away pondering many questions, a reaction shared by most of Martel's readers.

Orson Scott Card's *Ender's Game*

At the end of the audio recording of *Ender's Game*, released as part of a twentieth-year celebration of the book's publication, Orson Scott Card shares some of the history of the book, along with his ideas about differences between science fiction and fantasy. He laughingly says, "It's a matter of rivets versus trees." If the cover of a book shows trees, it is a fantasy, but if it shows rivets holding pieces of metal together, then it is science fiction.

When readers pick up a book with rivets on the cover, they know that they are stepping into a futuristic world as in *Ender's Game*, *Ender's Shadow*, and *Children of the Mind*. In *Ender's Game*, the book on which we are focusing, parents are allowed to have only two children. However, upon special application, those with "smart" genes can be given permission to have a third child, if they agree to "give" one of their children to the government if needed. Ender is the third child born to the Wiggin family. Questions are asked early on about whether his parents were truly converted to the policy or whether they just wanted another child. Ender is told that his father comes from a big Catholic family and was christened John Paul Wieczorek, while his mother comes from a Mormon family. Both of these religions encourage large families, but at age sixteen Ender's father invokes "the Noncomplying Families Act to separate himself from his family" (22). He changes his name, renounces his religion, and vows never to have more than two children.

Ender is told this when at age six he is taken away for primary training at Battle School in the Belt. He is also told that even though his father denies his Polish ancestry "since Poland is still a noncompliant nation, and under international sanction because of it," Mr. Wiggin has secretly baptized and given each of his children a legitimate saints' name (22). The authorities learned this information through computerized monitors placed at the base of the brain in each of the preschool Wiggin children. The book begins when Ender is six years old and the monitor is being removed from the back of his neck. This removal is generally interpreted as the sign that the government is no longer interested in a particular child.

On the day that Ender has his monitor removed, the old teasing begins and a bully named Stilson says, "Hey, Third, hey, turd, you flunked out, huh?" (6). He goes on to get the other boys to laugh and chime in with "Lost your birdie, Thirdie. Lost your birdie, Thirdie!"(6). When they begin to push Ender back and forth between them while chanting,

"See-saw, Marjorie daw."
"Tennis!"
"Ping-pong!"

Ender realizes this game is not going to have a happy ending. He decides that he does not want to be the one who will be "unhappiest at the end" (6) and so he grabs at Stilson's arm but misses. Stilson responds, "Oh, gonna fight me, huh? Gonna fight me, Thirdie?" (7).

Ender looks at the crowd and laughingly says, "You mean it takes this many of you to fight one Third?" The others step back and Ender kicks out "high and hard, catching Stilson square in the breastbone." Both he and Ender are surprised. Stilson was not really expecting to fight, and suddenly Ender realizes that Stilson and his gang will be after vengeance tomorrow. He thinks, "I have to win this now, and for all time or I'll fight it every day and it will get worse and worse" (7). He knows it is not manly to strike an opponent when he is down, and so Ender uses his feet to kick Stilson in the most tender parts of his body. The next morning, Colonel Hyrum Graff arrives at the door to interview Ender as to why he gave Stilson such a beating. The outcome is that Ender leaves with Hyrum Graff to enroll in the Battle School in the Belt.

The oldest son, Peter, is as smart as Ender, but he has so many "killer" and self-centered instincts that he is not chosen for Battle School. The appropriately named Valentine is also unusually smart, but she is too loving and kind to become a warrior. She is the one who at age two gave her baby brother the name of Ender because she could not pronounce Andrew.

Card's editor of the short story that eventually became the now-famous book wanted the title to be "Professional Soldier," but Card insisted on keeping "Ender's Game" because he had devised the name to allude to the "endgame" in chess. The name is especially well chosen because readers more familiar with football than chess can get a similar idea by thinking of an "end run." It also fits Ender's position as the last of the children in his family. And on Ender's first day at Battle School when he meets the other launchies (new kids) and explains how he got his name, one boy responds, "Not a bad name here. Ender. Finisher. Hey" (42).

An all-important video game that Ender plays is called *The End of the World*. And readers undoubtedly think of the boy's name near the climax when his teacher warns:

"If you can be destroyed I can do it."
"So I'm not the first."
"No, of course you're not. But you're the last." (277)

Other names that Card probably created to suggest multiple meanings include that of Hyram Graff. *Hire 'em* describes his job as a recruitment officer, while Graff might remind readers of the unsavory connotations of *graft*. Ender sometimes calls his main teacher Jailer Rackham, because of the control he keeps over Ender. His real name is Mazer Rackham, and he is the only officer to ever beat a bugger army. His first name sounds like *major* while having the harsh sound of *razor*. His surname might make readers think of a torture rack or of the way pool players "rack 'em up" before breaking or hitting the balls.

Near the end of the book, Ender, and in fact the whole world, learns that Ender has actually killed, rather than just injured, two of the boys he fought when they were bullying him. Their prophetic surnames names were Stilson and Bonzo (pronounced "Bone-so"). Ender learns how to pronounce Bonzo's name on the first day he is sent to join Salamander Army and told to report to Commander Bonzo Madrid. "Not bahn-zoe, pisshead," the commander tells him. "Bone-so. The name's Spanish. Bonzo Madrid. Aqui nosotros hablamos español, Señor Gran Fedor" (75).

Nearly all of the boys have nicknames that are at least "in your face" if not out-and-out hateful. Among the boys' names are Scorpion, Spider, Flame, Tide, Fly Molo, and Crazy Tom. Even Petra Arkanian, a girl who is well liked, is sometimes called Baby Butt, but also Petra the Poet. The Greek meaning of her name, "rock or stone," fits with the kind of support she gives to Ender.

When Ender watches Bernard, one of his tormentors, make fun of a new kid named Shen, he decides to do something about it. Bernard accuses the boy of having a butt that "wriggles," and as the poor boy storms off, Bernard calls, "Look at his *butt*. See ya, Worm!" (49). Ender goes on his computer and creates a nonexistent student that he names God. He uses the new account to send out a flashing message to all the students' computers:

COVER YOUR BUTT. BERNARD IS WATCHING.
—GOD (50)

Bernard goes red with anger and demands to know "who did this!" He figures out it must have been Ender and sends an accusatory note, but Ender already has his next message ready to send:

I LOVE YOUR BUTT. LET ME KISS IT.
—BERNARD (51)

While the event earns Ender an enemy, it earns Bernard a new nickname: Buttwatcher—"Just Watcher in front of the teachers . . ." (52).

At Battle School, the various armies are named after animals ranging from such fairly small and harmless species as Rabbits, Squirrels, Rats, Salamanders, and Hounds to the more dangerous Centipedes,

Leopards, and Tigers. More exotic names are the Asp Army, named for the small, venomous snakes of Egypt usually thought to be cobras, and the Condor Army, named for the large American vulture. The Griffin Army is named for the mythological creature whose head, foreparts, and wings resemble an eagle, but whose body, hind legs and tail resemble a lion. The Manticore Army is named for a fourteenth-century legendary creature with the head of a man, the body of a lion, and the tail of a dragon or scorpion.

Near the end of his training when Ender is being given increasingly difficult challenges, he is assigned to be commander of Dragon Army, even though there is no such army. The Dragon Army was disbanded four years earlier because in the history of Battle School, no team under the name of Dragon Army has ever won even one-third of its games. It is unclear whether or not the adult leaders believe in this kind of "name magic," but they are a practical sort and because they have a surplus of Dragon Army uniforms they decide to test out both Ender and the name by assigning him to start a new army. Ender will not be able to keep any of his present soldiers, nor will he be able to trade. Instead, as Graff explains, he is being given "the equivalent of an entire launch course," more or less the freshman class, and assigned the color code of grey, orange, grey (156–57).

Writers of science fiction and fantasy have an advantage in that they can sometimes get away with vague descriptions such as when Graff explains to Ender that the Buggers had no communication devices on their ships because their communication was instantaneous, from "body to body, mind to mind" (249). It took the humans seventy years to come up with something similar called the ansible. The name given to the human invention is Philotic Parallax Instantaneous Communicator, but as Mazer Rackham explains someone found the word *ansible* in an old book and that is the name that caught on. Of course people would prefer the name *ansible* because it is one word instead of four and it begins like *answer* and ends like *audible*.

Card created similarly suggestive names for political and military positions, as shown in the following chart, where we have made guesses as to what words and ideas Card wanted to trigger in the minds of his readers.

Political Terms Used in *Ender's Game*

Ender's Game Use and Meaning	Similar English Word(s)	Real World Meanings of the English Words
Hegemon (chief leader of the alliance)	hegemony hegemonic	Preponderant influence or authority over others. Domination or domineering.
Strategos (chief military commander of the I.F. defense)	stratagem strategy strategize strategic	An artifice or trick in war for deceiving and outwitting an enemy. To plan cleverly, that is to scheme.
Polemarch (chief adviser of the military fleet)	poleax

Poland

march marching | A battle-ax with a short handle and often a hook or spike opposite the blade. To attack, strike, or fell with, or as if with, a poleax. The country of Poland was identified in chapter 3 as a "noncompliant nation." Marching is a kind of human movement related to wars and armies. |
| Warsaw Pact (apparently a group in the alliance with unpopular ideas. Near the end Peter excludes them from what he calls the Locke Treaty.) | War

Pact | Because of its important role in World War II, the name Warsaw is especially likely to make people think of *war*. *Pact* is cognate with *pax* (peace) and *pangere* (to fix or fasten). |

Ender would not be very good at the kind of guessing that Card expects from his readers because Ender's life has been so focused that he does not recognize everyday allusions. The tool that Ender uses to defeat the Buggers is a Molecular Detachment Device, which causes substances to destroy themselves. It is commonly referred to as the Doctor Device. When Ender asks Mazer Rackham about this name, Rackham explains that it was first called by its initials, the M. D. Device. These initials are unknown to Ender, and so Mazer Rackam explains that it's a joke because the initials also stand for Medical Doctor. Ender misses the irony and hence the humor (273).

Historical allusions are easier for Ender to understand because his schooling consists of the regularly expected subjects, plus the military ones. As Ender alights from his initial flight to Battle School, Graff tells him that his job is not to be a friend, but to produce the best soldiers in the world.

> We need a Napoleon. An Alexander. Except that Napoleon lost in the end, and Alexander flamed out and died young. We need a Julius Caesar, except that he made himself dictator, and died for it. My job is to produce such a creature. (34)

Chapter 7 begins with readers overhearing a conversation between the adults, one of whom is worried because the children "aren't *normal*. They act like—history. Napoleon and Wellington, Caesar and Brutus" (67). Much later, Valentine makes a historical comparison when she is having one of her rare visits with Ender. Their conversation naturally turns to their older brother, Peter. Valentine explains to Ender that Peter thinks he is Alexander the Great. Then she asks, "Why shouldn't he be? Why shouldn't you be too?" (236). When Ender protests that they can't both be Alexander, Valentine reassures him that they can be two faces of the same coin and she can be the metal in between.

But even as she says it, she wonders if it is true because she has joined Peter in writing what today would be called political blogs and has fallen under Peter's influence. They manage to get onto the general citizen's access Internet where at first they use "throwaway names," but then settle into Valentine writing under the name of Demosthenes, who from 384–322 BC was a spokesman for military preparedness in Athens, and Peter writing under the name of Locke (1632–1704), the English philosopher known as "the father of empiricism."

Bean is a young boy who is much like Ender. On the day he shows up in Ender's newly organized Dragon Army, Ender says, "Name, kid?"

"This soldier's name is Bean, sir."

When Ender asks, "Get that for size or for brains?" (160), the other boys laugh, but Ender soon comes to respect Bean's brains and integrity, and they become buddies. The book *Ender's Shadow* tells basically the same story as *Ender's Game*, but from Bean's perspective. Among the insulting names that Ender is called are Bugger Wugger, Bastard, Fart Eater, Pinbrain, Pin Prick, Scrunch Face, and Maladroit. This last name comes from Bernard, who says even his own name with a French accent, because the French will not let their children begin studying "Standard" until the age of four, by which time French-language patterns will be set in their brains.

Other ways that Card reflects the international makeup of the I.F. is by having a Chinese student named Han Tzu but called Hot Soup and a Muslim named Alai, who when adults are taking notes on the students participating in Ender's voluntary extra training sessions, shouts out, "Hey . . . Make sure you spell my name right!" (112). When Ender is promoted early from his group of launchies, he is put into the Rat Army, whose commander is a Jewish boy named Rosen. He calls himself "Rose de Nose, Jewboy extraordinaire" (99) and tells Ender that

"Your practice sessions with half-assed little Launchies are over, Wiggin. Done. You're in a big boys' army now. I'm putting you in Dink Meeker's toon. From now on, as far as you're concerned, Dink Meeker is God."

"Then who are you?"

"The personnel officer who hired God," Rose grinned. (100)

Because of a myth that Jewish generals do not lose battles, the I.F. always appoints Jews to be the strategos. Rose's Rat Army is often "called the Kike Force, half in praise, half in parody of Mazer Rackham's Strike Force" (100). Those who resent the racial preferences like to remember that in the Second Invasion when an American Jew was hegemon, an Israeli Jew strategos, and a Russian Jew polemarch, "it was Mazer Rackham, a little-known, twice-court-martialled, half-Maori New Zealander whose Strike Force broke up and finally destroyed the bugger fleet in the actions around Saturn" (100). Based on this evidence, people say it does not matter who is a Jew, "but it did matter, and Rose the Nose knew it. He mocked himself to forestall the mocking comments of anti-semites" (100).

In this ugly atmosphere, Ender is happy to discover that his group leader is Dink Meeker, a boy with the most humble name of all the soldiers in Battle School. Dink proves with his humanity and his straight thinking to be anything but small and meek. He lets Ender know that he asked for him, and he teaches Ender one of his most valuable lessons: "Commanders have just as much authority as you let them have. The more you obey them, the more power they have over you" (102).

Among the ironies in the book is that Card refers to the army platoons as toons, a name which today, thanks to the 1988 film, *Who Framed Roger Rabbit,* is most likely to make people think of cartoons. Another irony is that the name of the war game Buggers and Astronauts scans the same as Cowboys and Indians, although the connotations are hardly the same. After we wrote a draft of this chapter in which we mentioned that *bugger* came into English during the 1500s from Bulgaria and that country's association with the Bogomils, who were thought to be sodomites, we communicated with Card through e-mail (November 30, 2006). He told us that when he wrote *Ender's Game,* he knew the term *bugger* "only in the innocent phrase *little bugger*" as used in such remarks as "Isn't that just like the little buggers?" The allusion was to "children, with only mild contempt mixed with vague affection (or at least the possibility of affection)." He wrote that it seemed to him that *bugger,* in the sense that he knew it, was "an obvious term" to adopt for an "enemy with insectoid features." Only after the book appeared and he was criticized for "homophobia" did he learn that the word "HAD the other meaning."

This is almost as ironic as the intended irony in his book when he had the buggers turn out to be real bugs who, even though they were physically separated from each other and their queen, had about as much will to control their individual behavior as do the cells in people's bodies, which is why they did not need speech or writing to communicate with each other. The biggest irony of all is that Ender's game is not a game. It turns out to be the real thing in which the world is saved by an eleven-year-old boy, who then has to figure out what to do with the rest of his life.

Another interesting thing that Card told us about his naming processes was that he gave no particular thought to choosing Mazer Rackham's name. He took his given name from the first president of Brigham Young University (Karl G. Maeser) where Card was working at the time, and his last name from the famous illustrator Arthur Rackham. He said he "could have chosen any number of different names for reasons just as arbitrary" but this combination *felt* right.

Why? Those decisions always come down to criteria that I'm simply not conscious of. In fact, I knowingly trust my unconscious to be smarter than I am. I prefer to go by gut reaction to things like names rather than any particular plan. Even when I name allegorically (or seemingly allegorically) as in *Hart's Hope* or the Alvin Maker books, it still has to feel like a name to me—it has to feel right. And it also helps me shape the character.

So it's quite possible that Mazer Rackham behaved as he did—tormenting Ender as part of his training—precisely because I was making the unconscious association of the *Rack* in *Rackham* with the tortures of the inquisition. In other words, it's possible that the name influenced the story, rather than the other way around. (I had not planned Mazer's interaction with Ender. In fact, when I made Mazer the hero of the first war, I had *no* plan to introduce him as a still-living character. He was supposed to be legendary. But I got to a point in the short story where I needed Ender to change teachers—and when I had this enigmatic guy show up in his room, I thought: What if this new teacher is Mazer Rackham himself? Cool! So there was certainly no plan there—the name really was part of creating the character.)

Card closed his e-mail communication by observing that interactions between names and authorial intentions, whether conscious or subconscious, are so complicated that they cannot be reduced to a simple "the author meant this," but yet it is fascinating to speculate and to compare the ideas that names trigger in the minds of readers especially when they are a surprise to the author.

Ursula K. Le Guin's *Tehanu*

Names are at the heart of the stories in Ursula K. Le Guin's Earthsea books. In the fantasy world created by Le Guin, the main characters—those who are aspiring to become magicians or sages—have three names over the course of their lives. As with many of the motifs in fantasy, the idea is a formalized extension of what happens in real life where infants often have "baby names," which get dropped when they go to school, where they are known by more grown-up versions of their names or by descriptive nicknames. When people leave school and move out into the public arena, many choose more professional-sounding forms of their own name or even create brand-new names for themselves. And depending on their roles in life, they might be called such names as Uncle Milton, Aunt Maggie, Mr. Jimenez, Dr. Bowen, and Professor Kaftan, or in religious settings, Elder Thompson, Father Kirkham, Sister Caroline, or Brother Frazier. As shown by the discomfort that feminists have expressed over naming practices associated with marriage, strong emotional attachments are connected to people's names.

In Le Guin's books the name changes serve as symbols of significant differences in the progression and the maturity of her characters. At birth, people are given a child name, and as they grow they might also have a nickname. However, the important naming event is when they are told their true or sacred name as when the boy Sparrowhawk learns that he is the archmage Ged, and the girl or woman known as Goha learns that she is the wise woman Tenar. These sacred names are known only to themselves and perhaps to the one or two people they choose to tell. The names are considered a great treasure and are what individuals will be known by after they die.

Here we are focusing on *Tehanu*, because it is one of Le Guin's more recent Earthsea books and has the added perspective of being told not from the perspective of the powerful, as were *A Wizard of Earthsea*, *The Tombs of Atuan*, and *The Farthest Shore*, but from that of a seemingly insignificant village woman and a terribly abused child, who by the end of the book will be known as Tehanu, the girl ordained to be the next archmage. On page 1, readers meet the woman called Goha, whose other name is Tenar. She is newly widowed and has decided to stay on her farm, at least until her daughter, who has married a merchant of Valmouth, has children and might need her help. Her grown son has gone to sea as a merchant sailor. Goha, brought from Kargish to Gont in Middle Valley by her husband, Flint, was rumored to have been important, or maybe even a witch, in her home country, and perhaps she was. The villagers notice that the great mage Ogion sometimes stops to visit with her, but then he visits "all sorts of nobodies" and so that isn't really proof (1).

Her husband called her Goha, after a little white spider. The name fit because she is talented at spinning fleece and wool into yarn and unlike her neighbors, she has fair skin. The villagers mostly have names taken from nature. Goha's daughter is named Apple, her son is named Spark, the shepherd who works for her is named Clearbrook, a healer who lives some distance away is named Beech, while the local healer is named Ivy, and neighbors living near Ogion on the Overfell include Aunty Moss and Heather, the goat herder.

It is a bad time in Middle Valley. People are forgetting the old teachings and wicked things are happening. This unfortunate state is made clear to Goha when her neighbor friend Lark (whose name no longer fits her body) comes asking for help—or mainly for comfort—because a terribly burned child has been found, apparently left behind by a group of traveling tramps. The child is probably six or seven years old, but when she was picked up from the remains of the fire she weighed no more than would a two- or three-year-old. Goha surmises that the girl's father had beaten her, and then, assuming that she was dead, threw her into the fire to destroy evidence of his wickedness. A younger man from the group came to Lark's house and said, "The child's not well. . . . She hurt herself, lighting the fire" and then disappears (3). He probably pulled the girl from the fire and left her lying on the ground before rushing off to catch up with the others. When Goha sees the child, she says, "Even Ogion couldn't heal this" (5). But then she takes the child's left hand in her own and speaking in Kardish says, "I served them and I left them. . . . I will not let them have you" (6).

The next chapter, "Going to the Falcon's Nest," begins a year later with readers' learning that the child, now called Therru, which means "burned," is under Goha's care. A traveling sheep dealer named Townsend comes to her farm, and after making sure she is the widow Goha, tells her that the mage of Re Albi is sick and has sent for her. He is surprised at how quickly Goha and the child, whom he can't bear to look at, are ready to go. The walk is long, partly because Therru tires easily and Goha cannot carry her for long distances. At night, they sleep at the side of the road but hidden among bushes. Midday, they meet a group of ruffians who, fortunately, are frightened away by Goha's commanding presence and Therru's appearance. But in an ominous foreshadowing, one of them with a face that looks "sick and stricken" stares and turns as if to follow them until his mates call, "Come on, Handy" (20).

For readers, the most significant part of the journey is that Goha tells stories to Therru, and in one of them explains the naming practices that are such an important part of the Earthsea books. She tells Therru about people having child names, use-names, and maybe a nickname too:

> You're my Therru, but maybe you'll have a Hardic use-name when you get older. But also, when you come into your womanhood, you will, if all be rightly done, be given your true name. It will be given you by one of true power, a wizard or a mage, because that is their power, their art—naming. And that's the name you'll maybe never tell another person, because your own self is in your true name. It is your strength, your power; but to another it is risk and burden, only to be given in utmost need and trust. But a great mage, knowing all names, may know it without your telling him. (12)

When Goha and Therru arrive at the mage's house, they find him alone (he has sent everyone away). He is very near death but makes an effort to notice Therru and to urge Goha (who he calls Tenar) to teach Therru well. Then he asks for Goha's help to get to the place at the edge of the woods where he wants to die. When they are there, he "laid his hand on hers; she bent down to him; he spoke his name to her, so that after death he might be truly known" (28). Several townspeople come to watch through the night with Tenar and to burn sweet oils and a wax candle in a glass. The next morning, the wizard of Gont Port arrives, and also the wizard of Re Albi. These two important men argue with only slightly restrained selfishness and pride over where Ogion should be buried. The older of the men sadly laments that although he walked all night he arrived too late, which means that "he must be buried nameless. . . . A great loss made greater!" (31). Tenar speaks up to tell the men that "his name was Aihal" and that he wishes to be buried where he now lies. The men are surprised at her speaking and one from Gont Port stares and asks who she is. When she responds, "I'm called Flint's widow, Goha. . . . Who I am is your business to know, I think. But not mine to say" (31).

Re Albi cautions her about how she speaks to "men of power" (31). Then, Gont Port recognizes her and acknowledges that she was once Ogion's ward. "And friend," Tenar adds, quickly apologizing for her words by explaining that she is very tired and has had a long night. Aunty Moss steps in to say that Goha was sent for and that Ogion waited for her to come before he would die. The older man looks at

Goha and says in amazement, "And . . . and he told you . . . ?" Tenar
finishes the sentence for him with "His name." The older man is in-
credulous, the younger one contemptuous. Tenar is angry and asks,
"Must I repeat it to you?"(32).

> "Oh!" she said. "This is a bad time—a time when even such a name can
> go unheard, can fall like a stone! Is listening not power? Listen, then: his
> name was Aihal. His name in death is Aihal. In the songs he will be
> known as Aihal of Gont. If there are songs to be made anymore. He was
> a silent man. Now he's very silent. Maybe there will be no songs." (32)

The book ends with an even more dramatic naming incident in
which Therru is given her name of Tehanu by the dragon Kalessin.
Therru calls the dragon to save Ged and Tenar, who were lured back to
the Overfill with a story about Aunty Moss needing Tenar. It is true that
Aunty Moss needs help, as Therru learns when she slips away to see the
woman while Ged and Tenar continue on up the hill. An important
sign of Therru's power is that she can call Aunty Moss by her true name
of Hatha. An even more important sign is that when the evil men are
about to push Ged and Tenar over the cliff, Therru uses the language of
the mages to call Kalessin, the magical dragon whose "nostril pits, big as
kettles, were bright with fire" and wisps of curling smoke (277). When
Kalessin saves Ged and Tenar, Ged says in the dragon's language, "Our
thanks, Eldest." And Kalessin responds "in the huge voice like a broom
of metal dragged across a gong: 'Aro Tehanu?'" Tenar, who had been
practically in a dead faint, suddenly looks around for "her child" Therru.
The girl is running toward Tenar and Tenar calls for her not to run, because she can see only from the side of her face that is not burned. Tenar
fears that she will misjudge or lose her balance and fall from the cliff. But
before Tenar can communicate the message, Therru is in her arms and
Ged suddenly understands who called Kalessin.

The newly named Tehanu speaks with the dragon in her language.
She is given the choice of whether to return to the dragon's land or to
stay on Earth with Tenar and Ged. She decides to stay, because Tenar
and Ged must stay in their own world, and now as the newly chosen
archmage, Tehanu has work to do. But first all three of them must go
and care for Aunty Moss.

CHAPTER SIX

~

Names to Reveal Ethnic Values: Amy Tan, Sandra Cisneros, Maya Angelou, Cynthia Kadohata, Sherman Alexie, and Others

The words *ethnic, ethnicity,* and *ethos* came into English from the Greek word *ethnikos,* which means "nation" or "people." In modern usage, the term usually refers to the classification of groups of people according to common racial, national, tribal, religious, linguistic, or cultural origins or backgrounds. Ethnic-related ideas commonly treated in young adult literature include characters'

- Developing pride in their heritage and ethnicity.
- Feeling disadvantaged because of their ethnicity.
- Resenting labels applied to them from outside of their own group.
- Facing challenges in crossing social barriers between ethnic groups.
- Having attitudes different from their parents' ideas about assimilating into mainstream culture.

Ethnicity is an especially important concept in the United States, because we are a country made up largely of immigrants, and we at least aspire to the idea that people are free to choose their own religions and to raise their social status through education and hard work, both of which relate in some ways to ethnicity.

In real life, people's names are lexically packed, meaning that they usually carry information about one's gender and in more subtle ways about one's racial ethnicity, the era in which a person was born, the attitudes and aspirations of the person's parents, and, if the person has a nickname, what kind of friends he or she has. In fiction, this is even more likely to be true because authors purposely design their characters' names to reveal such matters.

As this chapter shows, a surprising number of authors have discovered the efficiency of using both names and the practices surrounding naming customs to reveal attitudes connected with ethnicity. These attitudes range from mild surprise to out-and-out hostility and racism. Because there are so many variations among ethnic groups, and because in today's "global village" there is considerable intermixing among various groups, there is no end to the possibilities. As an illustration of the variety, we are presenting a sampling of name-related incidents from books written by authors who are especially well known for their representation of particular ethnic groups. Then, as a further illustration of the variety, we will conclude with briefer descriptions of several other books in which the authors (or their publishers) have included an ethnic name or allusion in the book's title as a way of signaling the content to potential readers.

Jeff Valdez is a Hispanic comedian who gets laughs of recognition from audiences when he tells them that his "brothers' names are Alfonso, Lorenzo, Ramon . . . [and me] Jeff. I guess that was right about the time my parents assimilated . . . right there!" His audience laughs because nearly everyone has in some way been touched by questions relating to assimilation, and we've all wondered what our parents were thinking when they named us.

Amy Tan's *The Joy Luck Club*

In English classes, many teenagers have read the short story, "Rules of the Game," excerpted from Amy Tan's *The Joy Luck Club*. A number of them go on to read the whole book in which Tan tells the story of four Chinese American mothers and their daughters, including the chess-playing

Waverly and her mother, Lindo, the two protagonists in "Rules of the Game." Tan first introduces readers to Waverly's older brothers, Winston and Vincent. They have such "American" names that they lead readers to believe that from the beginning the family was trying to assimilate. Then, when readers learn that Waverly was named for the street the family lived on, they feel a little sorry about her parents' naïveté, but still they think the family was trying to become "American."

Only near the end of the book when Lindo and Waverly are having one of their first noncompetitive conversations do we learn that Lindo named her first son Winston because she "liked the meaning of those two words *wins ton*." She "wanted to raise a son who would win many things, praise, money, a good life" (302). Two years later when another boy came along, she named him Vincent "which sounds like *win cent*, the sound of making money, because I was beginning to think we did not have enough" (303). By the time, their daughter was born, Lindo had become dissatisfied with her life and wanted everything to be better for this daughter who looked so much like herself.

> I wanted you to have the best circumstances, the best character. I didn't want you to regret anything. And that's why I named you Waverly. It was the name of the street we lived on. And I wanted you to think, This is where I belong. But I also knew if I named you after this street, soon you would grow up, leave this place, and take a piece of me with you. (303)

We quoted these two examples to show how, with the extra space available to them, authors can explore more of the individual subtleties that are involved in ethnicity than can stand-up comedians or reporters writing about immigration patterns and changing attitudes. Tan showed that while the Jongs did not give their children Chinese names, the matter was much more complicated than a simple *yes* or *no* to the idea of assimilation.

Another example from the *The Joy Luck Club* occurs when Waverly has been married and divorced, and is bringing her thoroughly "American" fiancé (an accountant named Rich, who has red hair and freckles) to meet her parents. As they say good-bye to her mother and father, Waverly is horrified when Rich calls her parents Linda and Tom and then firmly shakes "hands with that same familiarity he used with nervous new clients." As Waverly explains, "My parents' names are

Lindo and Tin Jong, and nobody, except a few older family friends, ever calls them by their first names" (198).

The next day she returns alone to her parents' apartment to check out their feelings. In a defensive mood, she is prepared to accuse her mother of disapproving and undermining her engagement, but her anger melts away when her mother awakes from a nap on the couch with

> "*Shemma?* Meimei-ah? Is that you?"
> I was speechless. She had not called me Meimei, my childhood name in many years. She sat up and the lines in her face returned, only now they seemed less harsh, soft creases of worry. "Why are you here? Why are you crying? Something has happened!" (200)

Waverly is suddenly touched by her mother's vulnerability as well as her strength and they have an "almost normal" conversation (202). At the end, Waverly sees her mother in a new light: "an old woman, a wok for her armor, a knitting needle for her sword, getting a little crabby as she waited patiently for her daughter to invite her in" (204).

Sandra Cisneros's *The House on Mango Street*

Sandra Cisneros's *The House on Mango Street* is a series of vignettes about a young girl growing up in the Latino section of Chicago. It was published for a general adult audience in 1983 but has since worked its way up to become a part of what is generally considered "the canon" in contemporary young adult literature.

Twenty-one out of the forty-six chapter titles are based on the names of people or places. The place names differ in style from the one that is used as the title of the book with such names as "Gil's Furniture Bought and Sold" and "Alicia & I Talking on Edna's Steps." The titles taken from people's names vary from "Edna's Ruthie" to "Rafaela Who Drinks Coconut & Papaya Juice on Tuesdays" and from "Minerva Who Writes Poems" to "Louie, His Cousin & His Other Cousin." The surnames in the book are easily identified as Latino: Cordero, Guerrero, Ortiz, and Vargas, while the first names include Alma, Armando, Blanca, Elenita, Geraldo, Izaura, Marin, Noreida, Raul, Refugia, Tito, Yolanda, Uncle Nacho, and both Angel and Angelo.

Meme Ortiz's real name is Juan, but when the neighborhood kids asked him his name "he said Meme, and that's what everybody calls him except his mother." He is best known for having a sheepdog "with gray eyes . . . and two names, one in English and one in Spanish" (23). Aunt Lupe was really named Guadalupe "and she was pretty like my mother. Dark. Good to look at. In her Joan Crawford dress and swimmer's legs" (58). "Mamacita is the big mama of the man across the street, third-floor front. Rachel says her name ought to be *Mamasota*, but I think that's mean" (76).

Before the family came to Mango Street, they had lived on Paulina, on Keeler, on the third floor of a house on Loomis, plus some other places that the narrator can't remember, even though she knows they will always be a part of her. By the time the family gets to Mango Street there are six of them and "everyone has to share a bedroom—Mama and Papa, Carlos and Kiki, me and Nenny" (3–4). Halfway through the story entitled, "My Name," which comes early in the book, the narrator tells readers that her name is Esperanza.

> In English my name means hope. In Spanish it means too many letters. It means sadness, it means waiting. It is like the number nine. A muddy color. It is the Mexican records my father plays on Sunday morning when he is shaving, songs like sobbing. (10)

After Esperanza tells the story of her great-grandmother who had the same name, she explains that at school they say her name funny, "as if the syllables were made out of tin," while in Spanish it is made out of "a softer something, like silver." She is jealous that her sister Magdalena can come home and become Nenny while she has to stay Esperanza:

> I would like to baptize myself under a new name, a name more like the real me, the one nobody sees. Esperanza as Lisandra or Maritza or Zeze the X. Yes. Something like Zeze the X will do. (10)

In the next story, when Esperanza meets Lucy and Rachel and they ask what her name is, she is thrown into her same old wish, but this time she adds the possibility of being Cassandra or Alexis, and is almost surprised when she tells them Esperanza and "they don't laugh" (15).

The kids in the neighborhood enjoy naming things, including their "First Annual Tarzan Jumping Contest," which Meme won "and broke both arms" (23). One of the neighborhood sayings is that "A woman's place is sleeping so she can wake up early with the tortilla star" (31), which means that mothers need to rise with the Morning Star to roll out the day's tortillas. One day when Esmeralda is showing off her knowledge of cumulus clouds, Nenny asks about a particular cloud and Esmeralda answers:

> "That's cumulus too. They're all cumulus today. Cumulus, cumulus, cumulus."
>
> "No," she says, "That there is Nancy, otherwise known as Pig-eye. And over there her cousin Mildred, and the little Joey, Marco, Nareida and Sue." (36)

In a later story, Ruthie points to a few clouds: "Look, Marlon Brando. Or a sphinx winking. Or my left shoe" (68).

The saddest story in the whole collection is the one named "Geraldo No Last Name." Marin is a girl who loves to dance and so she goes to lots of dance halls including the Uptown, the Logan, the Embassy, the Palmer, the Aragon, the Fontana, and the Manor. She "knows how to do cumbias and salsas and rancheras even." Geraldo was "just someone she danced with" never dreaming that she would be the last one to see him alive:

> An accident, don't you know. Hit-and-run . . .
>
> They never knew about the two-room flats and sleeping rooms he rented, the weekly money orders sent home, the currency exchange. How could they?
>
> His name was Geraldo. And his home is in another country. The ones he left behind are far away, will wonder, shrug, remember. Geraldo—he went north . . . we never heard from him again. (66)

Maya Angelou's *I Know Why the Caged Bird Sings*

One of the stories that Maya Angelou tells in chapter 16 of *I Know Why the Caged Bird Sings* does a wonderful job of explaining why she and everyone she knew "had a hellish horror of being 'called out of his name.'" It was considered an insult because of the centuries that Negroes had "been called niggers, jigs, dinges, blackbirds, crows, boots and spooks" (109). At the time, Maya, whose name given to her at birth was Margueritte Annie Johnson, and who in the story goes by Margaret, is twelve years old and is still traumatized by having been raped. She hardly speaks and is sent off to work with Miss Glory, a friend of her mother's, who has been a maid in Mrs. Cullinan's house for twenty years. Margaret's mother is hoping that the work will be therapeutic for Margaret and that it will also help her learn the ways of a white woman's kitchen in preparation for getting a job of her own.

Margaret has been working for several weeks and feeling sorry for Mrs. Cullinan because she does not have children of her own and so has to send Margaret on "a thousand errands from her back door to the back door of her friends. Poor old Mrs. Cullinan" (107). Then one evening, Mrs. Cullinan asks Margaret to serve her friends on the back porch.

The "speckle-faced woman" asks, "What's your name, girl?" and Mrs. Cullinan explains, "She doesn't talk much. Her name's Margaret." When the woman asks if she's "dumb," Mrs. Cullinan says, "No. As I understand it, she can talk when she wants to but she's usually quiet as a little mouse. Aren't you, Margaret?" (107).

Mrs. Cullinan adds that Margaret is a "sweet little thing," to which her friend replies, "Well, that may be, but the name's too long. I'd never bother myself. I'd call her Mary if I was you" (107).

And so starts a running battle. Miss Glory is on Margaret's side, at least in the beginning, and even Mrs. Cullinan sags a little when she says, "I want Mary to go down to Mrs. Randall's and take her some soup. She's not been feeling well for a few days" (108).

Miss Glory's face was a wonder to see. "You mean Margaret, Ma'am. Her name's Margaret."

"That's too long. She's Mary from now on. Heat that soup from last night and put it in the china tureen and, Mary, I want you to carry it carefully" (108–9).

Miss Glory walks the newly named "Mary" to the back door and confides, "Twenty years. I wasn't much older than you. My name used to be Hallelujah. That's what Ma named me, but my mistress give me 'Glory,' and it stuck. I likes it better too." (109)

Margaret doesn't know whether she "would laugh (imagine being named Hallelujah) or cry (imagine letting some white woman rename you for her convenience)" (109). She is so angry that she does not do either, but for the next week she leaves bits of egg yolk on the dishes and doesn't really "polish" the silverware. Miss Glory ignores her bad behavior. Then Margaret consults with Bailey, her brother, and together they come up with an idea. The next day, when Margaret is serving Mrs. Cullinan's friends, she drops the serving tray, and when Mrs. Cullinan shouts "Mary!" she picks up Mrs. Cullinan's favorite casserole dish (it is shaped like a fish) plus two green glass coffee cups, and as soon as Mrs. Cullinan comes around the corner she lets them fall on the floor (110).

Such a commotion ensues that Margaret is unable to explain the sequence of events to Bailey without bursting into laughter. The one thing she remembers clearly is that when the woman who originally insisted on calling her Mary says, "Who did it, Viola? Was it Mary? Who did it?"

Mrs. Cullinan says, "Her name's Margaret, goddam it, her name's Margaret!" Then she throws a wedge of the broken crockery at Margaret, but because she is so upset, her aim is off and it catches Miss Glory right over her ear and she starts screaming. As Margaret makes her exit she leaves the door wide open so all the neighbors can hear, and she smugly says to herself, "Mrs. Cullinan was right about one thing. My name wasn't Mary" (111).

Cynthia Kadohata's *Weedflower*

Cynthia Kadohata's *Weedflower* is the story of Sumiko, a young Japanese American girl living in California during the years leading up to World War II. Her parents were killed in an automobile accident and she and her brother, Takao (a.k.a. Tak-Tak), have lived for several years with Auntie and Uncle and their two almost adult sons, Ichiro and Bull. They have a flower farm, and Sumiko has several jobs, including heating the bathwater each day and disbudding the flowers, which means breaking off the smaller or defective buds so that the plant can concentrate its energy on the more perfect blooms.

The story begins when prejudice is just beginning to build against the Japanese, and soon Sumiko's uncle and her grandfather are arrested and taken with other community leaders to a camp in North Dakota. Within a few months, all of the Japanese families are moved from their homes, first to the San Carlos Race Track and eventually to the Colorado River Relocation Center (also called Poston) located on a Mohave Indian reservation near Parker, Arizona. While the story is fictional, Kadohata set the story at this particular center because this is where her father was interned. A couple of other camps were located on Indian reservations, but the Poston camp was the only one run by Native Americans and so was the most likely to have the kind of interaction that Kadohata writes about.

On Sumiko's first night at the camp, she is nervous and unable to settle down and sleep on her cot, which has been placed outside where it will be cooler. Then "a huge, beautiful moth fluttered around the cot and then flew away" (115). This helps Sumiko because she imagines that it is a visit from the spirit of her mother, whose name, Mayu, means "cocoon" and implies "nurturing" and "transformation." The image is a comfort to Sumiko because Jiichan, her grandfather, has always told her that "by staying very still" a larva changes itself from "being the ugliest thing in the world to the most beautiful" (115).

To Sumiko, the most beautiful thing would be to own her own flower shop and to be surrounded by flowers all day, to fill out invoices, and to arrange beautiful bouquets and window displays. As part of this dream, she has decided to name her first daughter Hanako, which means "flower child" (116).

Within a few days of being at the camp, Sumiko makes friends with a girl named Sachi, and together they go to look at the bean fields, which have been planted by people who got to the camp earlier than Sumiko's family. The green foliage is like a miracle in the dry desert. Suddenly Sachi hisses, "Shh! Hide!" Three Indian boys are also exploring the bean field, and Sachi explains that "they're not supposed to be in our camp. If they catch us, we'll get scalped. . . . After they scalp us, they'll cut off our fingers and boil them" (121).

Then, the girls hear a rattlesnake. Sachi screams and runs, but Sumiko trips on the vines and finds herself sitting "on her rear end a foot from the snake," which rises in the air and hisses. A calm voice says, "Walk back slowly. *Slowly*. It doesn't want to hurt you," and someone from behind lifts her onto her feet and partly walks/drags her backwards.

"Were you just going to sit there until it bit you?" asks a Mohave boy who appears to be about her age (122). He is named Frank, and throughout the story is a secret friend, although they see each other only rarely. A boy called Hook comes up and tells the other boys that they need to get home. The boy has a hook sticking out "from his left arm where a hand should have been, and Sumiko is surprised at how casually they call him Hook. In her culture, this would have been like "calling Mr. Moto [a partially blind neighbor at the camp] One Eye. If a Japanese person had a hook for a hand, you would act like the hook wasn't even there and get all embarrassed if you got caught staring at it" (123).

Kadohata uses various names to illustrate the emotions running through Camp Poston. One day when Sumiko and Frank are talking, Sumiko asks Frank if he isn't frightened about his two older brothers going to war. With a touch of bravado, he tells her, "Oh, no, they'll kill about a hundred Germans or Japs . . ." (215). Then in embarrassment his voice trails off and he apologizes, "I meant they'll kill the enemy. . . . I mean, you're not the enemy . . ." (216). Sumiko reminds herself that "everybody in America said 'Japs'—*everybody*. Even some Japanese said it. But hearing it from Frank sounded awful" (216).

One of Sumiko's neighbors is called an *inu*, which means "dog" because he was judged to be a snitch. Sumiko hears him being beaten one night because just after a woman had told him she had a camera, her barrack is raided and her personal belongings confiscated. Sumiko works hard to carry buckets of water to help the elderly Mr. Moto build a garden in front of their barracks, but still she can't find the energy to write a letter to her Uncle Hatsumi, who chides her about becoming *namakemono*, a "lazy bones" (137).

Because the people in the camp have been so abruptly separated from all their possessions and acquaintances, as well as the management of their own lives, many of the adults suffer from depression. Those who simply sit outside in their chairs, moving them from place to place as the sun travels across the sky, are called "shadeseekers," while those who position their chairs in breezeways between the barracks are called "windchasers."

As the war grows more intense, the government asks the residents of Poston to sign a loyalty oath as well as a statement of their willingness to join the American army. Those who decline to sign are sent to another camp at Tule Lake, California, which will no longer be considered a relocation center, but a segregation center. "Everyone called the men being shipped to Tule Lake 'No-No Boys'" (227). People from Tule Lake who answered *yes* on the forms are transferred to the Colorado River Center, so Sumiko has some new neighbors.

One of the happier naming incidents occurs early in the book when the family is getting ready to leave for wherever they will be placed. They can each take only what they can carry, and at the last minute Sumiko runs back into the shed with the idea of taking some of their flower seeds. She finds an envelope marked "Sumiko Strain," and happily tucks it inside her blouse. She is thrilled that Uncle Hatsumi thought enough of her to name one of his best strains of seeds after her and she takes seriously the responsibility of keeping this strain alive.

Near the end of the book, just before her cousin Bull leaves the camp to go into the army, he and Sumiko walk away from the big farewell party to talk outside. Sumiko has a wild thought. "Someday if you have a baby, can I pick out the name?" Fortunately, Bull is wiser than to say either *yes* or *no*. He tells her, "I'll have to see what my wife thinks about that. But maybe" (240).

Sumiko is trying to envision a future for Bull after the war. She easily imagines Ichiro, her "playboy" uncle "raising the kids she knew he would have" and wearing "dapper old-man clothes," but she can only imagine Bull "in his uniform but nothing beyond that. She shook off the thought" and told Bull she would write once a week and also send him lots of magazines to read (241). "He smiled one of his rare big smiles and pulled her close against his wide chest. 'Sumi-chan,' he said quietly" using the form of her name that means something like "dear one" or "beloved" (241).

The flowers that Sumiko loves the best are the *kusabana* (stocks, in English), which she explains to Frank are "weedflowers," meaning they grow in fields rather than in the more protected greenhouses. Sumiko speaks so lovingly about the smell and the colors of these weedflowers, especially when there is a whole field of them, that Frank chooses to call her Weedflower rather than Sumiko. In retaliation, she calls him Woodchopper.

Earlier, when she asks him why he and his friends have "American" names, she is surprised to be told that it is because the government does not want them to have "Indian" names. But at the very end of the book, she learns that in fact Frank does have an Indian name. She begs Mr. Moto for the best of the carvings he made for their garden so she can have a going-away present for Frank. It is a samurai soldier, which she puts in a box, along with papers on irrigation from Bull, and a note telling Frank the time she will be leaving in three days. She places the box in the tunnel of bean plants where she and Frank sometimes visit. She is disappointed not to hear from him, but just before the bus leaves, he comes riding up on his bicycle, bringing her a silver bracelet that his mother says he can give to her and also a small note that she reads on the bus after both the lonely boy on his bicycle and the camp are out of sight. In the note he tells her his Indian name: "Huulas, which means 'lightning.' His last name was Butler" (256).

Sherman Alexie's *The Lone Ranger and Tonto Fistfight in Heaven*

Sherman Alexie came to the attention of the general public with his 1998 award-winning motion picture *Smoke Signals*, which was based on the short stories in his book *The Lone Ranger and Tonto Fistfight in Heaven*. The title comes from the Lone Ranger radio show, which between 1933 and 1954 presented nearly three thousand shows. It was later adapted into a television program that ran between 1949 and, 1957, into several comic books and movie serials, and, as late as 1990, into a video game. The hero was a masked cowboy (sort of a Superman in rodeo clothes) always accompanied by an Indian named Tonto, who served as his all-around companion and man friday. *Tonto*, with this spelling but a slightly different pronunciation, means "stupid" or "foolish" in Spanish.

Both of us remember the show from our own childhoods, especially the catch phrases, "Who was that masked man?" and "Hi ho, Silver, away!" which we parodied into "Hi ho, Silverware" when we were assigned to set the table for dinner. We did not know the meaning of Tonto's name, but we nevertheless recognized the program's inherent racism and one of the few jokes that we remember from the time period was about the Lone Ranger and Tonto being surprised by a band of hostile Indians. The Ranger says, "Oh, now we're in trouble!" and Tonto replies, "What you mean WE, Paleface?"

Alexie does not belabor this point, but uses it to set the tone of his book when in the preface he writes:

> This book could have easily been titled *The Lone Ranger and Tonto Get Drunk, Fistfight, and Then Fall into Each Other's Arms and Confess Their Undying Platonic Love for Each Other in Heaven Followed by a Long Evening of Hot Dog Regurgitation and Public Urination.* (xviii)

Alexie's stories are set on the Coeur d'Alene Indian Reservation in northern Idaho, and although they were published for adults, many teenagers are reading them. While they deal with such serious problems as alcoholism, alienation, and broken dreams, Alexie brings in considerable humor to serve as a balance. And while not all Native Americans approve of the way that Alexie uses Indian naming patterns for humor, college students, both Native and non-Native, regularly ask Alleen to include Sherman Alexie stories in her young adult literature classes, while Don's students in sociolinguistic classes like to write papers on Alexie's use of language. Alexie is so popular among high school students that he was invited to be one of the featured speakers at the 2006 National Council of Teachers of English annual convention.

One of his techniques is to surprise readers by putting names together in unexpected ways, as when the story "Indian Education" is told by a boy named Junior Polatkin. Junior has such a miserable time in school that he reminisces about first grade and explains: "I was always falling down; my Indian name was Junior Falls Down. Sometimes it was Bloody Nose or Steal-His-Lunch. Once, it was Cries-Like-a-White-Boy, even though none of us had seen a white boy cry" (172).

By second grade, Junior is more assertive. When his teacher sends a letter home saying that his braids should be cut as a matter of respect, or he should withdraw from school, his parents come to school the next day and drag their braids across the teacher's desk.

"indian, indian, indian." She said it without capitalization. She called me "indian, indian, indian."

And I said, *Yes, I am. I am Indian. Indian, I am.* (173)

Near the end of the book, Junior dreams that he is a gunfighter with braids and a ribbon shirt. He doesn't speak English, but just whispers Spokane as he guns down Wild Bill Hickok, Bat Masterson, and even Billy the Kid. His name is Sonny Six-Gun and both "white and Indian people would sing ballads about him" (232).

Just before Christmas, Rosemary Morning Dove gives birth to a boy who she names _____,

which is unpronounceable in Indian and English, but means "He Who Crawls Silently Through the Grass with a Small Bow and One Bad Arrow Hunting for Enough Deer to Feed the Whole Tribe."

We just called him James. (110–11)

Characters who appear in some of the sadder stories with sadder names include the tribal chairman, David WalksAlong, who "walked along with BIA policy so willingly that he took to calling his wife a savage in polyester pants" (94). Dirty Joe got his name because he cruised the taverns at closing time and "drank all the half empties" (54). When Victor and his father can't find any food in the house, he calls his father Hunger and his father calls him Pang. Tremble Dancer is one of "the Urbans," or city Indians who has come back to the reservation after catching one of the white man's diseases. She has "burns and scars over her legs. When she dances around the fire at night, she shakes from the pain" (105).

The story "Flight" is a tragedy about John-John and his brother, "ace jet pilot Joseph Victor, code name Geronimo," who is reported to have been captured and taken prisoner during a routine military action. John-John waits by the window watching for his brother to come home, but the story he tells himself at nights just before he falls asleep is a comic routine that he and Joseph used to have over breakfast during happier times:

"Hey, John-John, why do you got two first names?"

"'Cuz you have to say anything twice to make it true?"

"No, that ain't it."

"Cuz our parents really meant it when they named me?"
"I don't think so."
"Maybe it's just a memory device?"
"Who knows?" . . .
"'Cuz I'm supposed to be twins?"
"No, man, that's too easy."
"'Cuz Mother always stuttered?" (229–30)

Another sad story is entitled "The Approximate Size of My Favorite Tumor." James Many Horses, who, depending on his mood, Simon also calls "little Jimmy One-Horse" or "little Jimmy Sixteen-and-One-Half-Horses," has cancer. When he tells Simon about his doctor showing him the X-rays, he describes his favorite tumor as being about the size and the shape of a baseball, complete with stitch marks.

"You're full of shit."
"No, really. I told her to call me Babe Ruth. Or Roger Maris. Maybe even Hank Aaron 'cause there must have been about 755 damn tumors inside me. Then I told her I was going to Cooperstown and sit right down in the lobby of the Hall of Fame. Make myself a new exhibit, you know? Pin my X-rays to my chest and point out the tumors. What a dedicated baseball fan! What a sacrifice for the national pastime!" (157)

At this, Simon calls him "little Jimmy Zero-Horses." Later, when the hospital releases Jimmy to die at home, he sits at his kitchen table writing letters to his loved ones on special reservation stationery that reads "FROM THE DEATH BED OF JAMES MANY HORSES, III." He explains that he says "DEATH BED" because "DEATH TABLE just doesn't have the necessary music." Also, he is the only James Many Horses, but he has added III to his name because "there is a certain dignity to any kind of artificial tradition" (168).

Other YA Books Where Names Open Doors to Considerations of Ethnicity

The Astonishing Life of Octavian Nothing: Traitor to the Nation, Vol. 1: The Pox Party by M. T. Anderson

This winner of the 2006 National Book Award for young readers is set near Boston in the 1770s in an institution named the Novanglian College of Lucidity, a name that can be roughly translated as the "New England College of Enlightenment." The American revolutionary spirit of the time vies for attention with what in an "Author's Note" is described as "provincial and incompetent" imitations of educational and philosophical experiments being carried on in Europe, similar to those that Jonathan Swift satirized in his "The Academy of Lagado." As part of their desire for objectivity, the scholars are identified by numbers rather than by names; however, Octavian and his mother have names because they are part of an experiment. Octavian's mother, who in Western Africa was a young and beautiful princess of the Egba people, is named Cassiopeia, after the mythological daughter of Arabus, who married the king of Ethiopia and was turned into a constellation. Octavian's first name makes him sound almost like a Roman emperor, while the "nothing" part shows how some of the scholars think of him when their experiment goes badly. The scholars are raising Octavian under optimal conditions and are having him educated by the best minds in hopes of proving that an African boy is not really capable of classical learning. One of his first clues to his status comes from an older black boy, a servant named Bono, who is as close to being a friend as Octavian has. Bono, who calls Octavian Prince O, does not like his own name. When Octavian asks him why not, he says because it was given to him as a jest:

> I was in my mother's womb when she was bought. My maser purchased me and her, one price. My name's Pro Bono. For free. They got two, my mother and me, for the price of one. (39)

Octavian does not know what to say, especially after Bono says, "You and your mama were a single lot. See?" Octavian argues that "My mother is a princess," to which Bono says, "Your mother was a princess." By the end of the book, Octavian's mother has died from smallpox, and he has run away. In these adventures, he goes by the name of Prince, but when he is captured, he is called Octavian Gitney, a name he refuses to respond to because of his hatred for Mr. Gitney, the man more or less in charge of the college and its experiments.

Colibrí by Ann Cameron

Cameron's book is set in contemporary Guatemala. Its title is the Spanish translation of the name of twelve-year-old Tzunun Chumil, whose

Mayan name means "Hummingbird Star." Throughout most of the book the girl thinks she is Rosa Garcia, the name she has been given by "Uncle" Baltasar, a man who kidnapped her because of a fortune-teller's prophecy that the girl would bring him riches.

Esperanza Rising by Pam Muñoz Ryan

Ryan based her lyrical book on the story of her own grandmother, the girl with the Spanish name of Esperanza. She is born on a prosperous ranch in Mexico, and in the 1930s is looking forward to a grand celebration of her thirteenth birthday. Then, her father is killed and his brothers, in effect, hold her mother hostage hoping that she will marry one of them so that they can be owners of the ranch. In desperation, Esperanza and her mother run away to California and become part of the multiethnic labor camps of the Great Depression. Esperanza rises not only to a change of country but also to a change of social class.

Jip: His Story by Katherine Paterson

Paterson's story is set in 1855–1856 in rural Vermont. Jip West is probably eleven or twelve years old. No one knows for sure because he was abandoned on West Hill Road when he was only two or three. The townspeople who found him named him Jip because his dark complexion made them think he might have fallen from a gypsy wagon. But when the story opens, Jip has learned that he did not fall from a gypsy wagon, but instead was abandoned by his mother, who was a runaway slave being taken back to the South. She left her half-white child behind in hopes that he would be rescued and allowed to grow up free, but now bounty hunters are out to get him and collect the one hundred dollar reward being offered for returning slaves to their owners.

Lizzie Bright and the Buckminster Boy by Gary D. Schmidt

One explanation of why at the turn of the last century Henry Ford's cars were called Tin Lizzies is that Lizzie was such a common name for African American housemaids that it seemed an appropriate name for Model T Fords, which were always black and worked hard during the week, but got polished and dressed up to go out on Sundays. Schmidt's book is the story of two preachers' kids—black, ragtag Lizzie Bright Griffin and white, thoroughly starched Turner Buckminster. Their

story is based on a real event on Malaga Island off the coast of Phippsburg, Maine. The island had been settled by runaway slaves, and when
the shipbuilding industry waned and the citizens of Phippsburg went
looking for a new way to make money, they settled on tourism. As part
of their plan, they felt they had to rid the island of its black residents.

The Meaning of Consuelo: A Novel by Judith Ortiz Cofer

Cofer's book, set in 1950s Puerto Rico, won the 2003 Award of the
Americas for a young adult book. Consuelo, whose name is cognate
with *console* and *caring for*, is the older daughter in a troubled family.
Her father is enchanted with all things American and wants to move
to New York. Consuelo's younger sister, who is the joy of her parents'
life, is named Mili, short for Milagro meaning "miracle." Consuelo
watches helplessly as Mili drifts into insanity and then into suicide.
Consuelo is left to decide whether she should stay and "console" her
family or move to New York and start her own life.

Monster by Walter Dean Myers

Monster is not really the boy's name; it is Steve Harmon, but Monster
is what the prosecutor calls him, and as he waits to go on trial for being an accessory to a crime, he keeps writing movie scripts in hopes of
figuring out just how appropriate the name is.

My Name Is Not Angelica by Scott O'Dell

O'Dell dedicated this historical novel "To Rosa Parks, who would not
sit in the back of the bus." It is the story of Raisha and her two friends,
Dondo and Kanje, who are put on a slave ship and taken to St.
Thomas. Dondo and Kanje's names are changed to Abraham and
Apollo, and Raisha's to Angelica. After participating in some of the is-
land revolts, the boys commit suicide rather than return to slavery, but
Raisha is pregnant and chooses to save her own life and the life of her
baby.

Name Me Nobody by Lois-Ann Yamanaka

The first three chapters in this novel, which is set among contemporary
Japanese Americans living in Hawaii, are entitled "Name Me," "War
Names," and "School Names." The protagonist's mother named her

Emmylou Harris, after her favorite singer. Then she skipped out when Emi-Lou was three, leaving the child to be raised by her grandmother. Emi-Lou is overweight and hates it at school when she is called Emi-lump, Emi-oink, or Em-fat. Later on when her best friend becomes friends with a lesbian, Emi-Lou is called Emi-lez.

Naming Maya by Uma Krishnaswami

If Maya's name does not tell readers that this story has something to do with India, the name of the author will probably do the job. Maya grew up in New Jersey, but now she finds herself back in India with her mother, who is intent on selling the family home after her parents' death. Maya's parents are divorced and it does not help the situation that Maya suspects their problems started with a disagreement over her name. By the end of the summer she has learned a lot of things about her heritage, including the fact that her parents' divorce has nothing to do with her.

Shabanu: Daughter of the Wind by Suzanne Fisher Staples

The eleven-year-old protagonist is named for the wind that blows across the Cholistan Desert in Pakistan. Shabanu loves helping to care for her nomadic family's herd of camels. Both she and her sister, Phulan, are betrothed, but when her sister's fiancé is killed, changes must be made, and Shabanu is promised to a wealthy landowner. The sequel Haveli (Knopf, 1993) also reveals much about ethnic beliefs and differences, even among people, who from an outsider's point of view, appear to be much the same.

Tyrell by Coe Booth

Booth's book stands out as one of the relatively few in which an ethnically marked boy's name is used in the title. Ty or Tyrell, an African American teen, lives in a homeless shelter in the Bronx, where the author has been a teacher and a social worker. His girlfriend, Novisha, works in a shelter run by Spanish-speaking immigrants from Cuba so there is plenty of cultural intermixing.

When My Name Was Keoko: A Novel of Korea in World War II by Linda Sue Park

As shown by Linda Sue Park's Newbery-winning A Single Shard, she is steeped in Korean history. However, When My Name Was Keoko is set in a much more recent time period than is *A Single Shard*. It was inspired by stories from family members who lived in South Korea between 1940 and 1945, when it was occupied by Japan, and Koreans were forced to adopt Japanese names and study the Japanese language. Alternating chapters are written by a girl who is trying to grow accustomed to her new name of Keoko, and her older brother who is adjusting to his new name of Sun-hee.

Zazoo by Richard Mosher

Mosher's mystical book found its way onto several 2001 honor lists. It is the story of a Vietnam orphan, who, when she was two years old, was brought "home" to a French village by one of the town's aging World War II "heroes." The man, whom the girl calls Grand-Pierre, tends the locks on the town's canals, and as thirteen-year-old Zazoo explains to a boy who arrives on a bicycle asking mysterious questions about people in the town, Grand-Pierre made up her name "while we were on our way here from Vietnam. Seems to fit, somehow. A girl like me who looks so different on the outside—I mean, who looks so Vietnamese . . ." The boy interrupts, "Yet on the inside is as French as anyone else?" (4).

~

CHAPTER SEVEN

Names to Build a Dual Audience: Daniel Handler and the Lemony Snicket Books

Audiotapes and CDs, released simultaneously with popular new books, are making children's literature a cross-media genre enjoyed by all ages. Our own grandchildren and their parents listen to recorded books not only on long car trips but on their way to school, tae kwon do, bowling, and wherever. While we are only occasionally in the same car, we enjoy listening to many of the same books. Our most successful cross-generational and cross-the-miles experience has been Daniel Handler's *A Series of Unfortunate Events*, which Handler[1] writes under the pseudonym of Lemony Snicket. Some of our college students compare the Lemony Snicket books to Matt Groening's *The Simpsons*, which is one of the few shows that whole families watch "without talking, reading, or fighting" because there is something in it for all ages, and viewers do not want to miss any of the allusions.[2]

The Lemony Snicket books tell the story—actually many stories— of the Baudelaire orphans, Violet, Klaus, and Sunny, and their never-ending struggle to keep Count Olaf (a distant relative) from stealing the fortune left in a trust for them by their deceased parents. As we have read and listened to these books, we've been impressed by how cleverly Handler creates and uses personal names, place names, and even common names as a way to intrigue adult and teen audiences, in addition to his primary audience of young readers. For example in *The Reptile Room* (Book the Second), the Baudelaires are thrilled because it appears that they will get to live with their Uncle Montgomery Montgomery, a well-known herpetologist, who tells them to call him Uncle Monty. Rather than spelling out a connection, Handler leaves it to his readers to think of the famous collector of snakes as Monty Python.

The first book, ironically titled *The Bad Beginning*, was published in 1999 with the thirteenth, *The End*, being released on Friday the thirteenth in October 2006. Children who were nine or ten when Book the First appeared were well into their teens by the time Book the Thirteenth came out. For the most part, Handler manages to retain his original readers, while picking up many more, by making his clever name games and allusions more challenging and by making the books fuller. Book the First has 163 pages, Book the Sixth has 260 pages, while Book the Twelfth has 354 pages and Book the Thirteenth has 369. We are not saying that length is the sole measure of sophistication, but it is part of it, and as we will show, Handler's allusions, especially those that come through the mouth of Sunny, the baby, also become increasingly complex.

Part of the charm of the books is that they are written and illustrated as old-fashioned melodramas. They have the exaggerated feel of the Victorian era, and of locations that, while not being futuristic science fiction nor old-world fantasy, are unlike places that readers have actually been. The books are printed on thick paper with generous white space. Each book has a frontispiece illustration, as was the fashion in publishing before World War II. Brett Helquist's additional small sketches go a long way toward establishing a playfully nostalgic tone, as do such character names as Carmelita Spats and Captain Widdershins and such place names as Salmonella Café and Briny Beach. Some of the Helquist sketches are of nameplates that characters use to give themselves credibility. For example, the first page of chapter 8 in *The Miserable Mill* (Book the Fourth) is decorated with the sign that hangs in front of Dr. Georgina Orwell's optometry office, while chapter 10 has a drawing of Sir's desk. He is the owner of the sawmill and as usual is hiding behind a cigar and a cloud of smoke and his "THE BOSS" nameplate (129).

As of 2006, most of the mass marketing was of hardbound books connected to all kinds of other media, including a major film, sound recordings, games, puzzles, activities, and miscellaneous supporting books. The books do not have book jackets; instead framed drawings of the orphans, always in a perilous situation, appear to be glued right onto the hardback bindings. The generic title of *A Series of Unfortunate Events* is worked into the upper part of the ornate frame, while "Book the . . . " and "by Lemony Snicket" is worked into the bottom of the frame with the individual titles being printed below the drawings. The insides of the book covers are lined with what looks like brocade cloth or embossed wallpaper, and the *Ex Libris* book plates, implying that the books are intended for personal ownership rather than for library checkouts, feature the innocent orphans in a round portrait at the top with the villainous Count Olaf, in an appropriate disguise, in a similar frame at the bottom. They are both surrounded by prickly vines.

Smart Allusions

Some educators worry that children will be confused by learning historical or literary names from a parody or a media allusion before they know what "the real thing" is. Rather than worrying about something we cannot control, we think it makes sense to simply share the fun with young readers so that they will come to understand literary processes variously referred to as recycling, intertextuality, or smart allusions. One of our favorite examples is Handler's naming of Klaus and Sunny Baudelaire, whose names sound enough like Claus and Sunny von Bulow to remind adult readers of the most famous murder case of the 1980s, in which the aristocratic Claus von Bulow was accused of injecting Sunny, his wealthy, diabetic wife with an overdose of insulin.

Klaus and Sunny's older sister, Violet, was named for "The Violet Hour" in T. S. Eliot's *The Wasteland*, a favorite poem of their parents, which near the beginning of *The Penultimate Peril* (Book the Twelfth) they are using to help figure out a coded message. They feel close to T. S. Eliot, not only because of their parents' fondness for him, but because in *The Austere Academy* (Book the Fifth), they attended the Prufrock Preparatory School, named after Eliot's "The Love Song of J. Alfred Prufrock." Their less-than-fond memories of the school include

Count Olaf, under the guise of a coach, forcing the Baudelaires to undergo S.O.R.E. (Special Orphan Running Exercises). While they are doing this, the other students are in late-night assemblies listening to the vice principal play his violin. He is a terrible musician named Nero.

The only good thing that happens at Prufrock Prep is that the Baudelaires meet two other orphans named Duncan and Isadora Quagmire. Young readers are amused at the family name of Quagmire, while adults are probably reminded of the American dancer Isadora Duncan, who became a tragic symbol of "the roaring twenties" when her neck was broken as she was jerked from the backseat of a speeding roadster because her long, elegant scarf got tangled in the open spokes of a wheel.

Duncan's untimely death inspired Gertrude Stein's mordant comment "Affectations can be dangerous." Besides amusing adult readers with allusions to ironic real-life events, Handler may be hinting that his melodramatic plots are not so far from real life as they first appear.

In addition to T. S. Eliot, Handler alludes to authors Herman Melville and Edgar A. Guest.[3] Melville makes his first appearance in *The Miserable Mill* when poor uncomplaining Phil gets his leg hopelessly mangled in the stamping machine and a fellow worker pulls out a coupon offering "fifty percent off a cast at the Ahab Memorial Hospital," named in honor of Melville's one-legged captain (97–98). In *The Austere Academy*, Violet, Klaus, and Sunny wear sports uniforms featuring a portrait of Herman Melville, while Count Olaf, disguised as Coach Genghis, wears an Edgar A. Guest shirt. In *The Grim Grotto*, readers are again reminded of Herman Melville because the small submarine that the children use in their escape is named the *Queequeg*, after the beautifully tattooed man who in *Moby Dick* makes himself a hand-carved coffin.

In *The Hostile Hospital* (Book the Eighth), the institution is appropriately named the Heimlich Hospital, because its purpose is to save lives. Klaus and Sunny go there with the V.F.D. (Volunteers Fighting Disease) to sing cheerful songs as they hand heart-shaped balloons to the patients. One of the patients, who has food poisoning, is named Emma Bovary (cf. Gustave Flaubert's *Madame Bovary*); another is Clarissa Dalloway (cf. Virginia Woolf's *Mrs. Dalloway*) "who did not seem to have anything wrong with her but was staring sadly out the window of Room 1308" (140).

For the beginning of *The Slippery Slope*, Handler cleverly alludes to Robert Frost, without naming him:

> A man of my acquaintance once wrote a poem called "The Road Less Traveled," describing a journey he took through the woods along a path most travelers never used. The poet found that the road less traveled was peaceful but quite lonely, and he was probably a bit nervous as he went along, because if anything happened on the road less traveled, the other travelers would be on the road more frequently traveled and so couldn't hear him as he cried for help. Sure enough, that poet is now dead. . . .
> The Baudelaire orphans however, had no choice but to be on the road less traveled. (1–2)

Snicket's allusions to Edgar Allan Poe include the children's surname of Baudelaire, which might remind adult readers—at least those who majored in literature—of Charles Pierre Baudelaire, the French poet who viewed Edgar Allan Poe as a kindred spirit and devoted himself to translating Poe's work into French. This simple fact is not enough to "prove" a connection but it becomes more credible when combined with the fact that one of the few characters to appear in every book is Mr. Poe, the incompetent bank official assigned to serve as the guardian of the children and their fortune. *The Vile Village* (Book the Seventh) is centered, both literally and figuratively, around the great Nevermore Tree, home to "a murder of crows," which Snicket compares to "a flock of geese, or a herd of cows, or a convention of orthodontists" (50). Although these thousands of menacing black birds are crows instead of ravens, knowledgeable readers can hardly keep from being reminded of Edgar Allan Poe's ". . . quoth the raven nevermore."

Handler names the eye doctor in *The Miserable Mill* Dr. Georgina Orwell, an allusion to George Orwell's *1984* because the doctor is also a hypnotist who manages to control Klaus's mind, at least temporarily. Esmé Squalor is the wife of Jerome Squalor, a distant cousin who in *The Ersatz Elevator* is assigned to be the children's guardian. Her name comes from the title of J. D. Salinger's short story, "To Esmé with Love and Squalor." Probably few readers make that connection, but still the name is memorable because of the surprise of someone as fashion conscious as Esmé putting up with the surname of Squalor. An extra little joke is that the address of the Squalor's penthouse is 667 Dark Avenue, which will be darker to those adults who recognize the number as being just one off from 666, the Sign of the Beast.

Place Names and Common Nouns

Snicket enjoys playing with word roots. He uses *mort*, from the Latin word for "death" in the name of the Mortmain (killer) Mountains. Mr. Poe works for the Mulctuary Money Management bank, which suggests Mortuary Money Management. The school motto at Prufrock Prep is "Memento Mori," intended to remind students of their impending deaths. The image is helped along by the shape of the school buildings, which are tall rectangles with rounded roofs so that the campus looks like a giant graveyard filled with tombstones. When Handler explains that *le petit mort* is a feeling that a little part of you has died, adults will be more likely to think of the phrase in connection with sexual orgasm.

One of the most complicated examples of playing with a place name comes in *The Wide Window* (Book the Third) when Count Olaf forces Aunt Josephine to write a suicide note. She fills it with grammatical and spelling mistakes, which he is too ignorant to recognize. But when the children, who know how much she values correct English, look carefully at the note and make a list of her "mistakes," they realize that she is being imprisoned in the Curdled Cave, and so they rush to her rescue.

Throughout the series, such place names as Hotel Denouement, Mount Fraught, and Grim River foreshadow coming events. While less imaginative authors would simply talk about such things as forests, fountains, and lakes, Handler never misses a chance to create an amusing name, as with Caligari Carnival, Damocles Dock, Finite Forest, Fowl Fountain, Grim Gorgonian Grotto, Hazy Harbor, Lake Lachrymose, Lavender Lighthouse, Rancorous Rocks, Rarely Ridden Road, Stricken Stream, and Wicked Whirlpool. With names such as the Fickle Ferry, Hurricane Herman, Lachrymose Leeches, and Lousy Lane, he opens a door to expanding on the ideas or treating them humorously. An example is when in *The Grim Grotto*, he writes about "the sinister smells of Lousy Lane, along which the children traveled long ago" (139). He then goes on to give a medical definition of *lousy*, which he warns will probably be needed if Count Olaf's hygiene gets worse. When he writes his explanatory definitions, which some readers hate but others love, he often includes the interesting names he has already introduced. For example, he explains that *lousy* sometimes means that something is "abundantly supplied, the way Count Olaf is lousy with treacherous plans or the *Queequeg* is lousy with metal pipes, or the entire world is lousy with unfathomable secrets" (140).

Even with common, as opposed to proper, names, Snicket plays with literal versus metaphorical meanings, as in *The Hostile Hospital* (Book the Eighth) he observes that "operating theaters are not nearly as popular as dramatic theaters, musical theaters, and movie theaters, and it is easy to see why" (189). In the same book, he explains that Esmé Squalor's high-fashion shoes keep sticking to the floor because their stiletto heels are "made with a small slender knife where each heel should be" (115). Our favorite Lemony Snicket vocabulary lesson comes from *The Ersatz Elevator*, which gets its title from a secret passageway disguised as an elevator shaft. We like Snicket's explanation mainly because it is so much better than our own feeble explanation of *ersatz* as "not real or a substitute," which we gave our grandchildren when we took them to lunch at a cafeteria and they wanted to know what was in a dish identified as "Ersatz Crab Salad." Snicket explains how when the Baudelaire children are imprisoned in the shaft of the *ersatz* elevator they escape from their ersatz guardian, Esmé Squalor, by making an ersatz rope from ties and sheets and pieces of clothing. The book ends with readers being told that they may imagine that Duncan and Isadora manage to free themselves from Count Olaf's clutches and that Violet, Klaus, and Sunny find a home and that Count Olaf gets arrested and sent to prison and that they all live happily ever after. But then comes the catch, as Snicket adds that such imaginings will all be ersatz, as are all imaginings (253).

Sunny's Contributions

One of Handler's clever inventions is the baby Sunny, whose unusually sharp front teeth serve as a *deux ex machina* to solve all kinds of physical problems faced by the protagonists. She helps them escape by biting

either the ropes or the hands that are holding them; she uncovers duplic-
ity by biting real body parts disguised as fake, and she even manages to
climb out of an elevator shaft by using her teeth as holding clamps. But
her real contribution to the series is how she saves Handler as an author.
In the early books, she makes one-syllable sounds, which Snicket inter-
prets as whatever will move the plot forward. For example, in *The Wide
Window* (Book the Third), she shrieks, "Toi!" and Snicket writes,

> By "Toi!" she probably meant "I have never eaten a peppermint because
> I suspect that I, like my siblings, am allergic to them," but it was hard to
> tell. She may also have meant "I wish I could bite a peppermint, because
> I like to bite things with my four sharp teeth, but I don't want to risk an
> allergic reaction." (5)

In *The Hostile Hospital*, Sunny has grown much more sophisticated,
both in her concepts and in the allusions she makes. The children are
trying to figure out who on a sheet of paper is being alluded to as Ana
Gram and Sunny shouts out "Orlando!" Snicket explains that Sunny is
thinking of the actor in Count Olaf's troupe "who looks like neither a
man nor a woman" (76). Adults, but not children, will recognize the
appropriateness of the transsexual character being named for the
gender-changing title character in Virginia Woolf's novel, *Orlando*.
    In *The Austere Academy*, when the children's new friend, Isadora,
says modestly that she writes poems, Sunny shrieks "Sappho!" which is
interpreted to mean something like "I'd be very pleased to hear a poem
of yours!" (45). Snicket is teasing adults with his reference to Sappho,
the talented teacher and poet on the ancient Greek island of Lesbos,
from which speakers created the word *lesbian*. As serendipity to the initial wordplay, the fortune left to Isadora and Duncan is a collection of
sapphires.
    As the books progress and Sunny grows older, her references become
more sophisticated and she takes on the task of explaining them. In *The
Penultimate Peril* (Book the Twelfth), the children have been working as
concierges in the Hotel Denouement in hopes of eavesdropping on the
guests and discovering what's going on. When they meet to report on
their various observations, they are terribly discouraged to find themselves as puzzled as ever. After some mental struggling, Sunny makes
them all feel better by remembering and calling out the name, John

Godfrey Saxe, which, of course, reminds the children of the famous American poet from Vermont who was much loved by their father, who used to recite Saxe's poem "The Blind Men and the Elephant." A blind man falls against the side of an elephant and concludes it is a wall. One of his companions feels the tusk and says it is a spear; another feels the trunk and thinks it is a large snake, while another recognizes the leg as a tree, and so on. Sunny is the one who remembers the poem and sees its relevance to their present situation because as the youngest child she most recently sat on their father's lap and listened to it.

Later in the hotel, Count Olaf is threatening to kill one of the hotel owners with a harpoon gun. The children interfere, but in the course of events, the harpoon projectile goes off and kills the man in spite of their efforts. When they are being accused of murdering him, Sunny says, "Henribergson," which, in an allusion to the famous French philosopher, means "It's more complicated than that," but no one pays any attention (248). Mob hysteria ensues, and a trial is quickly organized. In preparation for the trial, the children are allowed to take a short nap in a closet-sized room, and are surprised when they are awakened to be handed blindfolds. When they look surprised, the man says, "Everyone wears blindfolds at a High Court trial . . . except the judges, of course. Haven't you heard the expression 'Justice is blind'?" (267). Sunny responds with "Scalia," which Snicket explains means something like "It doesn't seem like the literal interpretation makes any sense" (268). However, her siblings do not think it wise to translate, and the court moves forward. Adults listening to the book along with young readers will probably make the same decision as did Violet and Klaus about not interrupting Snicket's story to explain this allusion to Supreme Court Justice Antonin Scalia, who is known for his insistence on literal interpretations.

Doppelgangers and Doubles

Throughout the series, Handler uses names to play with the fairly sophisticated literary concept of doppelgangers and doubles, which has a long history in tragicomic pieces. Some critics use the terms of *double* and *doppelganger* interchangeably, while others make a distinction that we think is helpful. Doubles are multiple concepts which develop from a single character or idea, while doppelgangers are two characters who are so alike that they are practically indistinguishable. Handler is apparently fascinated with the concept of people appearing in multiple versions, as shown first by Duncan and Isadora Quagmire's insistence that they be called triplets even though there are only two of them. Their brother, Quigley, is thought to have perished in the fire that killed the Quagmire parents. He actually escaped and made his way through an underground tunnel to Uncle Monty's reptile room, where he reads about the Baudelaires and sets off to find them in hopes that they can help him find Isadora and Duncan. The idea of two becoming three is repeated on an adult level in *The Penultimate Peril* with the discovery that the twins, Frank and Ernest, have an identical brother named Dewey.

Doppelgangers
Examples of dopplegangers include Tweedledum and Tweedledee in Lewis Carroll's *Alice in Wonderland*, Estragon and Vladimir in Samuel Beckett's *Waiting for Godot*, and Rosencrantz and Guildenstern in William Shakespeare's *Hamlet* and also in Tom Stoppard's *Rosencrantz and Guildenstern Are Dead*. Doppelgangers do not have to be identical in appearance, but they have to have enough in common to intrigue, or perhaps just confuse, reading or viewing audiences.

In *The Penultimate Peril*, the Baudelaires at last find their way to the Hotel Denouement, where they hope to solve the mystery of the meaning of the initials V. F. D. But even before entering the hotel, they have a doppelganger experience because the hotel is built hanging over a smooth lake which forms a perfect reflection of the hotel, including its name and all the numbers. When the Baudelaires finally realize that the hotel they are closest to is only a reflection and they look up to see the real hotel, they are surprised to see that on the actual building, the numbers and the names have all been reversed so that they are readable in the reflection, but not on the real hotel.

Before they go in, they are warned by Kit Snicket, a relative of Lemony's, that the hotel may not be safe after all because it has been infiltrated by their enemies. She tells them about two identical twin brothers, Frank and Ernest Denouement, who own and manage the hotel.

> "Frank will help you as best he can, but be very careful. The schism has turned many brothers into enemies. Under no circumstance should you reveal your true selves to Frank's treacherous identical brother Ernest."
>
> "Identical?" Violet repeated. "If they're identical, how can we tell them apart?"

Kit took one last sip of her coffee. "Please try to pay attention," she said. "You'll have to observe everyone you see, and make such judgements yourselves. That's the only way to tell a villain from a volunteer. Now, is everything perfectly clear?" (40)

The Baudelaires are never able to tell which one is Frank and which one is Ernest and so all their dealings are accompanied by such disclaimers as "Frank said, or maybe it was Ernest" (145), "Frank or Ernest replied" (68), and "said Frank in an annoyed voice, or Ernest in an irritated one" (61). Handler builds irony into the situation by giving the two brothers names with approximately the same meaning of "honest" or "candid," which neither of them is. Handler may also have wanted to remind readers of the plot of Oscar Wilde's *The Importance of Being Earnest*, in which much of the humor is based on the confusion over real and fake names.

Every few pages, someone at the hotel says to Violet or Klaus, "You are who I think you are, right?" Not knowing who is asking, Violet and Klaus respond with such ambiguous answers as "And are you who I think you are?" They are soon startled to meet a third identical brother named Dewey Denouement. He is a sub-sub librarian, meaning that he keeps his very secret library under the lake that is in front of the hotel. Although Ernest and Frank get all the public attention, Dewey is obviously the one who organized the hotel so that anyone who can find a book in a library will know how the hotel works because it is organized according to the Dewey decimal system.

When the children first meet Count Olaf, he is directing an acting troupe. Some of these same actors follow him into the carnival business, and then on into pursuing the Baudelaires and their fortune. Because of their abilities as actors and their supply of costumes and disguises, these characters are well suited to playing doppelganger roles. One example is the sinister couple referred to not with names but as "the man with a beard, but no hair" and "the woman with hair, but no beard." In *The Slippery Slope*, these two bring an unmistakable "aura of menace" when they arrive at the top of Mortmain Mountain dressed identically in fire-retardant suits (123). They have just come from burning the V. F. D. headquarters, formerly located on the mountain.

Another of Count Olaf's cronies is a bald-headed man with a long nose. He is the one who becomes Foreman Flacutono in *The Miserable*

Mill. Handler uses the technique of giving him a fake name that is an anagram of Count Olaf to show that he is a doppelganger or a clone who will do whatever Count Olaf wants him to do. In *The Hostile Hospital*, he keeps the name but changes the title to become Surgeon Flacutono, the inventor of the cranioectomy.

Another set of doppelgangers from the carnival are two women with white faces, which they keep powdering. In *The Hostile Hospital* they are disguised as doctors with the names of Tocuna and Flo. Again their names form an anagram of Count Olaf. Sunny and Klaus manage to steal their disguises and foil Count Olaf's plot. A third Count Olaf doppelganger is the hook-handed man who in *The Hostile Hospital* covers his hooks with surgical gloves and becomes Dr. O. Lucafont, another anagram taken from Count Olaf's name.

In *The Miserable Mill*, the owners are Charles and Sir, perhaps an allusion to basketball star Charles Barkley's nickname. Sir has no redeeming qualities, while Charles at least recognizes the inappropriateness of having children, especially a baby, work in a sawmill and of giving them only one meal a day, except for chewing gum at lunchtime. While Charles occasionally sneaks food to them—once a peach and another time a few raisins and a small piece of beef jerky—we still consider the two men to be doppelgangers because although they are full partners, Charles has nothing to say about the management of the mill, and in fact, would have been turned into boards and sawdust if it hadn't been for the Baudelaire's rescue of him.

Doubles

The idea of the literary double is that one character becomes two (sometimes more) individuals. Famous examples include Robert Louis Stevenson's *The Strange Case of Dr. Jekyll and Mr. Hyde*, Franz Kafka's Gregor Samsa in *The Metamorphosis*, Oscar Wilde's protagonist in *The Picture of Dorian Gray*, and Virginia Woolf's *Orlando*, a book which has already been mentioned in relation to one of the Caligari Carnival workers who was neither a man nor a woman.

Snicket is probably making an allusion in *The Miserable Mill* to the hero in James Thurber's "The Secret Life of Walter Mitty," who loved imagining himself saving the day. Thurber shows that Mitty is going into his dream world with the sound "ta-pocketapocketa." Handler does something similar when Klaus is trying to figure out how he can save Charles's life in the sawmill with nothing but chewing gum.

Hukkita—hukkita—hukkita! The machine began making the loudest and roughest sound Klaus had ever heard. Charles closed his eyes and Klaus knew that the blade must have hit the bottom of his foot. He grabbed a bigger handful of gum and shoved it into his mouth. (171)

Psychologically, the concept of the double is easier for people to relate to than the idea of doppelgangers because most of us have felt conflicting emotions and we know about schizophrenia and about people with multiple personalities. Claire Rosenfield has observed that the concept of duality has a long history of inspiring both terror and awe, as when twins are born or when people see reflections of themselves in water or in mirrors or when they see paintings or sculptures of themselves.[4] Another critic, C. F. Keppler, lists these common idioms that reflect people's almost subconscious feeling that there is more than one soul in a human body:

going to pieces,
being all broken up,
being beside oneself,
pulling oneself together,
falling apart,
going out of your mind,
getting a grip on yourself.[5]

In *The Hostile Hospital*, Violet becomes an unwilling double when she is drugged and registered at the hospital under the name of Laura V. Bleediotie, which is an anagram of her real name. Before Klaus and Sunny can rescue her from being the model patient in a live demonstration of a cranioectomy, they have to discover which of the names on the hospital records is an anagram. Luckily they have had lots of practice from figuring out the tricks that Count Olaf and his cronies have used to make new names for themselves. Count Olaf's distinguishing characteristics include a tattoo of a fearsome-looking eye on his left ankle and one long eyebrow that runs straight across his forehead. However, he is a master at disguising himself, as shown in the following chart outlining some of his doubles:

Count Olaf's Doubles in the Lemony Snicket Books

Book	Name	Explanation
Book the First *The Bad Beginning*	Al Funcoot	Count Olaf gives himself this pen name to hide the fact that he is the author of the play *The Marvelous Marriage*, through which he hopes to become Violet's husband and thereby the owner of the Baudelaire fortune. This is an anagram of his own name, but usually he gives himself a brand-new name.
Book the Third *The Wide Window*	Captain Sham	He hides as a sea captain with a peg leg covering his tattoo and an eye patch that partially covers his distinctive eyebrow. When he courts Aunt Josephine, she calls him Julio, Captain S., and J.
Book the Fourth *The Miserable Mill*	Shirley	Count Olaf grows long fingernails and wears long silk hose to play the role of a receptionist at the Paltryville sawmill. "She" explains that she is lonely and so desperately wants to adopt three children.
Book the Fifth *The Austere Academy*	Coach Genghis	As the school's coach, Count Olaf hides his eyebrow under a lopsided turban and his ankle tattoo under high-top gym shoes. He proves to be just as demanding as was the real Genghis Khan.
Book the Sixth *The Ersatz Elevator*	Guntar the Auctioneer	With the help of Esmé Squalor, Count Olaf tricks the children and their guardian Jerome Squalor when he sets himself up as an auctioneer.
Book the Seventh *The Vile Village*	Count Omar	This is the name used by the reporter for *The Daily Punctilio*, who also mistakenly calls the children Veronica, Klyde, and Susie.
Book the Twelfth *The Penultimate Peril*	Countie	Esmé Squalor uses this affectionate name for Count Olaf, who is her new boyfriend.

The fullest example of Snicket playing with doubles—really multiples—is the way he ties the various books together by creating dozens of meanings for the initials V. F. D. Early on, the Baudelaires are led to believe that these initials have something to do with the good people who might save them from Count Olaf and his cohorts. The first meaning that seems to make sense is Volunteer Fire Department, especially since both their parents and the Quagmire parents were killed in house fires, but then the Baudelaires find themselves visiting hospital patients as Volunteers Fighting Diseases. In *The Slippery Slope*, near the top of Mortmain Mountain they find the Valley of Four Drafts; they discover that a Vertical Flame Diversion is a chimney, that a Verse Fluctuation Declaration is a code, and that a Vernacularly Fastened Door has a combination lock that operates on language. By now, the Baudelaires have been joined by a very smart and helpful scout, who turns out to be Isadora and Duncan's lost brother, Quigley Quagmire. Together they figure out that to open the door they need to type in the name of the scientist credited with discovering gravity (SIRISAACNEWTON), the Latin name for "the Volunteer Feline Detectives" (PANTHERALEO), and the central theme of Leo Tolstoy's *Anna Karenina* (TRAGEDY) (147). When they type in the last word, the lock seems to stick and they begin wondering if maybe they misunderstood the theme of Tolstoy's book. After all, people who lead a "daring life of impulsive passion" end up doing all kinds of things (148). They briefly think of Adam and Eve and the result of their leading a life of impulsive passion and then of "Bonnie and Clyde, another famous couple who lived a daring life of impulsive passion" (148).

The Mystery of Beatrice

Through all of the books, Snicket keeps the name Beatrice exactly the same, but treats it in a different way in each book. She is the mysterious woman who in the dedications is the recipient of his fondest feelings. The humor comes in the way Snicket creates variations on the theme of missing her. He starts with alliteration and surprise: "To Beatrice—darling, dearest, dead." Then he plays with switching from literal to metaphorical meanings as in "For Beatrice—You will always be in my heart, in my mind, and in your grave." "For Beatrice—When we were together I felt breathless. Now you are," and "For Beatrice—Our love broke my heart, and stopped yours." Judging from Book the Twelfth, she died in a house fire as did the Baudelaire's parents: "No one could extinguish my love, or your house."

He uses contrast in "For Beatrice—When we met, my life began. Soon afterwards, yours ended," and comparison in "For Beatrice—Summer without you is as cold as winter. Winter without you is even colder." Book the Fourth has the longest dedication:

> To Beatrice—My love flew like a butterfly,
>   Until death swooped down like a bat.
>   As the poet Emma Montana McEllroy said:
>   "That's the end of that."

Books the Tenth and Eleventh, respectively, are perhaps the most enigmatic. "For Beatrice—When we met, you were pretty, and I was lonely. Now, I am pretty lonely," and "For Beatrice—Dead women tell no tales/ Sad men write them down."

Various websites give contradictory explanations of the name, but the one that most literary people are likely to think of is the one shared with us by Lisa Arter, one of our graduate students. She explained that in 1264 when Alighieri Dante was nine years old, he saw Beatrice Portinari and fell in love with her. Over the next sixteen years they would greet each other on the street, but from the age of twelve Dante was promised to Gemma di Manetto Donati. In 1290 when Dante and Beatrice were each twenty-five years old, Beatrice died and Dante took refuge in writing about his love for Beatrice and his concept of ideal love. *The Divine Comedy* was a memorial to Beatrice, who served as his guide through Paradise. He had a daughter with Gemma, who although she was named Antonia, took the name of Sister Beatrice when she became a nun.

Just as Handler promised, Book the Thirteenth ends ambiguously, and the last word in it is *Beatrice*. She appears to have been the mother of the Baudelaire children. Her exact relationship to Lemony Snicket is not quite explained, but the children do find out that her name is the one actually painted on the boat that they and Count Olaf are in when during a terrible storm they wash up on a mysterious island. They discover her name only after Count Olaf has pulled off a Carmelita Spatz taped-on sign to reveal his own taped-on sign, which the children pull off as they leave the island, still orphans and still in danger, but apparently not from Count Olaf.

On the island, they are greeted by a girl named Friday, who explains that she was born on the island after her mother landed there ten years earlier. She explains that the island is totally peaceful thanks to their "facilitator," who is named Ishmael, but who prefers to be called Ish. He is a man who both literally and figuratively has feet of clay. He sits on a kind of throne with his sore feet packed in clay. Besides learning about "feet of clay," the children learn the difference between a moral compass and a magnetic compass and between the fermenting of their ideas and feelings and the fermenting of the coconut milk that the islanders drink. Their lives are ironically saved by the very same lovable snake that Uncle Monty had jokingly named the Incredibly Deadly Viper, and as they leave the island without Count Olaf, "yet another question about their lives was answered, and yet another mystery had begun" (8 of the appended chapter 14).

Notes

1. In writing this chapter, we find ourselves using the name of Snicket when we are thinking of Daniel Handler as almost a character in the books, but as Handler when we are thinking of him as an outsider, that is, as the author behind the whole idea.

2. Owen, David, *TV Guide* cover story (January 3–9, 1998), cited in *Encyclopedia of 20th-Century American Humor* by Alleen Pace Nilsen and Don L. F. Nilsen. Phoenix: Oryx Press, 2000, 35.

3. Edgar A. Guest (1881–1959) is the poet whose books, including *A Heap O' Livin'* and *When Day Is Done*, were wildly popular during the first half of the twentieth century but were judged by literary critics to be overly sentimental. Judith Guest, author of the well-received *Ordinary People* (1976), is his great-niece.

4. Claire Rosenfield, "The Shadow Within: The Conscious and Unconscious Use of the Double," in *Stories of the Double* edited by Albert J. Guerard. New York: Lippincott, 1967, 311–30.

5. C. F. Keppler, *The Literature of the Second Self*. Tucson: University of Arizona Press, 1972.

CHAPTER EIGHT

~

Names as Memory Hooks: J. K. Rowling and the Harry Potter Books

In this chapter on memorable names, we are focusing on J. K. Rowling and her Harry Potter books both because of the length of her books and the number of characters she includes. Jim Dale, the actor who records the books, told a *New York Times* reporter that he had been forced to create 125 different voices when he recorded Book Four: *Harry Potter and the Goblet of Fire*. He was referring only to the characters with speaking parts. In addition to these more-or-less human characters, for each book Rowling devises dozens of other names including place names and names for purely imaginary things, including potions and spells.

The first book in her proposed series of seven was *Harry Potter and the Sorcerer's Stone* (Year 1) published in the United States by Scholastic in 1998, followed by *Harry Potter and the Chamber of Secrets* (Year 2) in 1999, *Harry Potter and the Prisoner of Azkaban* (Year 3) in 1999, *Harry Potter and the Goblet of Fire* (Year 4) in 2000, *Harry Potter and the Order of the Phoenix* (Year 5) in 2003, and *Harry Potter and the Half-Blood Prince* (Year 6) in 2005. The final volume, *Harry Potter and the Deathly Hallows*, telling the story of Harry's seventh year at Hogwarts School, is scheduled for release in July of 2007. The books have been translated into some thirty languages and have such a crossover audience between readers of all ages that each time a new book appears it shoots to the top of the *New York Times* general best-seller list.

Harry Potter is an orphan whose parents were killed by Lord Voldemort, more commonly referred to as "He-who-must-not-be named" and "You-know-who." In the struggle between good and evil, the Harry Potter books have similarities to J. R. R. Tolkien's Lord of the Rings books, C. S. Lewis's Chronicles of Narnia books, Philip Pullman's His Dark Materials trilogy, Ursula K. Le Guin's Wizard of Earthsea books, and even to the *Star Wars* movies. However, a major difference is that while J. K. Rowling is telling a serious story, she fills it with humor, much of which comes from the names she creates. Another difference, which underlies much of the humor, is that the world in which Harry operates is parallel to our own. Until Harry was twelve years old he was raised in a world of Muggles (nonmagical humans) by the Dursley family, which consists of Aunt Petunia, Uncle Vernon, and Cousin Dudley. On Harry's eleventh birthday, he is informed through messages delivered by owls from Professor Dumbledore, the head of the Hogwarts School for Wizards and Witches, that he is eligible for admission to the school. When Aunt Petunia and Uncle Vernon try in vain to ignore the increasingly urgent invitations, Hagrid, a half giant who is the gameskeeper, and later becomes the teacher of the Hogwarts class in the Care of Magical Creatures, comes to fetch Harry. Each book is the story of one year that Harry spends at the school. Important characters include various faculty members and Harry's best friends: Ron Weasley and the whole Weasley family, as well as Hermione Granger. His enemies are fellow students Draco Malfoy and Draco's two henchmen, Crabbe and Goyle, and in the adult world, Lord Voldemort and perhaps Professor Severus Snape.

Most authors who create imaginary worlds give their readers an assist by providing glossaries, but Rowling does not do this nor does she provide "catch-up" summaries at the beginnings of the new books. While the various books are much too complicated to summarize, what we will explore in this chapter are the techniques that Rowling uses to make her names memorable enough that they will stick in readers' minds not only for six hundred pages of a book, but also long afterwards because as the books have grown longer, the time in between their release has also increased. When readers pick up the "latest" Harry Potter book it may have been more than a year since they were reading about the characters. We will also look at how cleverly she uses Latin and Greek roots and allusions, which make her names not only easy for readers to understand and remember, but also easy for translators to communicate their "sense" in many other languages.

Descriptive Names

As shown throughout this book, authors frequently devise names to fit their characters by hinting at their appearances, personalities, or the roles being played. Rowling does this not only for character names, but for places, events, items, and imagined spells and charms. Such names serve a double purpose. First, they help an author develop characterization and ideas, and second, they remind readers who or what the author is referring to in subsequent mentions. J. K. Rowling does not need to be descriptive with such names as Harry, Ron, and Hermione because they play such important roles that readers do not need reminding of who they are, but descriptive names help with background characters.

At the simplest level are such animal names as Fang for Hagrid's dog and Fenrir Greyback for an especially vicious werewolf, and Number 12 Grimmauld Place as the address for the "grim, old" house that Harry inherits. Creatures known as the Inferi are "inferior" because they are little more than walking corpses. Faculty members at Hogwarts who are named for their appearance include Professor Flitwick, who is so short that he has to stand on a stack of books to see the class, and Mad-Eye Moody, who has one eye that spins around. Madame Olympe Maxime is a visiting head of school from France, who is "large-boned," actually part giant, as is Hagrid. Rowling uses Madame Maxime's *maximum* size to add a light touch to the somber funeral scene at the end of Book Six when she arrives and takes up two and a half of the folding chairs that had been set out on the lawn.

People's actions are more often a reason for their name. Professor Sprout teaches herbology, while Professor Binns is a *has-been*. He is a ghost who teaches history through deadly dull lectures because ever since he left his body in the chair in front of the fireplace, he has taught strictly from habit. Nearly Headless Nick is another ghost who has to wear shirts with high ruffled collars and hold his neck straight up to keep his head from dangling. His beheading had gone awry because the ax was dull and so had given him only a bad *nick*.

Personality characteristics are often foreshadowed by the names that Rowling chooses. For example, Harry's mother is named Lily, which most readers will recognize as a symbol of purity. Her hostile sister, who serves as Harry's foster mother, is named Petunia, which in the language of flowers symbolizes anger and resentment. Ludovic Bagman is in charge of the Department of Magical Games and Sports. His given name is cognate with *ludicrous* and the idea of "play," while his surname should have served as a warning to the Weasley twins, Fred and George. He convinced them to set up a gambling ring at a big Quidditch tournament, and then he "bagged" the money and ran off with it.

Professor Gilderoy Lockhart comes to Hogwarts in a great flourish of positive publicity, but long before the end of the year students realize that he is a fraud whose "royalty" is simply *gilded on* and whose heart is *locked* to any real emotion. Another prophetic name is that of Dolores Umbridge. She is the woman who in Book Five when Professor Dumbledore is temporarily banished is assigned to take over Hogwarts under the offensive title of high inquisitor. Her first name means "pains" or "sorrows" as seen in the name of the Via Dolorosa in Rome, which is the path that Christ walked when carrying the cross to the site of his execution. Her surname of Umbridge is just one letter off from *umbrage*, which in Latin means "shade" or "shadow" as seen in both *umbrella* and *somber*. *To take umbrage* at something is to have doubts or suspicions, which in their *doleful* way is exactly what the students feel towards Professor Umbridge.

The Malfoy family is Harry's nemesis. The family surname translates to something like "bad faith," with the first part being the same morpheme as in such negative words as *malice, malignant, malpractice,* and *malnourished*. Draco Malfoy is the first school bully that Harry meets, and as the story gets more complicated readers see Draco getting more Draconian while Draco's father, Lucius, gets more like Lucifer. Crabbe and Goyle are Draco's cobullies and as the story goes on Crabbe gets more "crabby," while Goyle gets more gargoyle-like.

Cornelius Fudge is the minister of magic, who throughout the books "fudges" the truth as he tries to keep control and stay in power. In Book

Six, he finally loses his job, but not before he has a major quarrel with Professor Dumbledore over his desire to enroll Harry as a kind of public relations spokesman whose job will be to reassure the public that his ministry is doing a good job. His replacement is Rufus Scrimgeour, who, with the same goal, takes every opportunity to involve Harry in verbal scrimmages. Scrimgeour's name might also remind readers of theater backdrops called *scrims*, which are opaque when a scene is lighted from in front of a scrim, but transparent when the light comes from behind.

At the beginning of Book Six, when the minister of magic feels obliged to pay a visit to the British prime minister, he informs the prime minister that his new assistant, Kingsley Shacklebolt, is in fact a highly skilled Auror, who is going to serve as the liaison or "connection" between the two worlds. David Colbert in *The Magical Worlds of Harry Potter* says that, in fact, *shacklebolt* is an old word for handcuffs, so in this sense the prime minister's new assistant is there to rein in or control his boss.

Hagrid is the half giant who first comes to fetch Harry from the Dursley's house. He has lived at Hogwarts since he was thirteen, and because Professor Dumbledore asked him to teach the Care of Magical Creatures class, he is officially part of the faculty. However, some faculty and staff members snub him because he is large and awkward as well as unrefined. While his name can be interpreted as someone who is "hag ridden," he personifies the dictionary definition of *haggard* because he is "untamed" and "wild in appearance." His awkwardness, however, is nothing compared to that of his half brother, Grawp, who is a full-blooded giant and whose name sounds like *grope* or *gawk*. In Book Six, at Professor Dumbledore's funeral, Rowling uses an incident with Grawp to break the terrible sadness after Hagrid carries Dumbledore's wrapped body to the front of the crowd and places it carefully on a table:

> Now he retreated down the aisle, blowing his nose with loud trumpeting noises that drew scandalized looks from some, including, Harry saw, Dolores Umbridge . . . but Harry knew that Dumbledore would not have cared. He tried to make a friendly gesture to Hagrid as he passed, but Hagrid's eyes were so swollen it was a wonder he could see where he was going. Harry glanced at the back row to which Hagrid was heading and realized what was guiding him, for there, dressed in a jacket and trousers each the size of a small marquee, was the giant Grawp, his great ugly boulderlike head bowed, docile, almost human. Hagrid sat down next to

his half-brother, and Grawp patted Hagrid hard on the head, so that his chair legs sank into the ground. Harry had a wonderful momentary urge to laugh. But then the music stopped, and he turned to face the front again. (643)

Spelling Innovations

The Harry Potter books are filled with "creative" spellings, which Rowling uses for several purposes. In relation to memory making, unique spellings force readers to slow down and figure out just which word Rowling has intended, and whether or not she has an underlying reason for a particular spelling. Only occasionally does she treat misspellings as misspellings. One of these rare occasions appears early in Book Six when both the former and the present ministers of magic (Cornelius Fudge and Rufus Scrimgeour) call on the prime minister of England to warn him that Lord Voldemort has returned and to reassure him that they will do all that is possible to protect the Muggles. Rowling tells in retrospect about an earlier visit when the prime minister remembers Fudge telling him about "Kwidditch (or that was what it had sounded like)" (9). In this case, Rowling was using what is called "eye-dialect," which is making a word "look" as if it is being spoken by someone who doesn't quite know the expected way of speaking.

Most of the time, Rowling uses unique spelling simply to remind her readers that they are "tourists" in a country not quite their own. This is what she is doing when she has Harry ride on the Knight Bus (rather than the Night Bus) and buy his school supplies at the Flourish and Botts bookstore. Hogwarts students drink Elderflower, instead of elderberry, wine and Butterbeer instead of root beer or buttermilk. They also mend their books with Spellotape, which has an advantage over Cellotape because it corrects spelling errors at the same time that it mends tears in their papers.

Probably the biggest advantage of Rowling's unusual spelling is that it serves as an invitation to readers to join in imagining different ideas that she hints at, as when she names the almost-out-of-control house elf that Harry inherits Kreacher, while the docile house elf who is happy to go about *daubing up* messes is named Dobby, and a poltergeist who is always making people feel *peeved* is named Peeves.

The name that Rowling chose for Floo Powder, which is what enables magicians to climb in a fireplace and be immediately transported to someone else's fireplace, is especially clever. She could have spelled it *Flue* because in people's houses that is what the travelers go through, or *Flew* as in the past tense of flying. But by using *Floo*, she left it to her readers to think of these two other possibilities as well as of the present tense *Flee*, which has the familiar ring of *Flea Powder*.

Another example of Rowling playing with a familiar-sounding phrase is her *Avadra Kedavra* destroyer curse, which according to Priscilla Spencer's website is Aramaic for "May the thing be destroyed." While it looks "different," it probably reminds most readers of the "magical" charm of *Abracadabra*, which they have already met through folktales.

Professor Dumbledore's Pensieve Bowl is a magical container where he stores memories. It is appropriate that the name sounds like *pensive* because this is the mood with which Dumbledore and Harry approach it when Dumbledore wishes to explain past events and to "teach" Harry what he is up against. The *sieve* spelling is also appropriate because Dumbledore uses the Pensieve Bowl to *sift* his memories and to figure out the importance of various events.

Spelling things backwards is another way to be creative, as when Harry discovers the Mirror of Erised (*desire* spelled backwards). When someone looks in the mirror, it reflects back to them what they most desire. In Harry's case, he sees himself standing with his parents, James and Lily. Hogwarts, the name of the school, is simply a reversal of the species name of *warthogs*, which are generally considered to be among the strangest and ugliest of all mammals.

Rowling gets even more creative with anagrams, as with the one that plays a big part in the plot of Book Two, *The Chamber of Secrets*. The story revolves around a mysterious student from the past named Tom Riddle. Ginny, the youngest of the Weasley children, is given his school notebook or diary. Throughout the year, she communicates with this mysterious former student and is drawn into his evil plans. It takes Harry's acquisition of the book and communication with its real owner to find out that the book belonged to Tom Marvolo Riddle, which is an anagram of *I Am Lord Voldemort*.

Near the end of Book Six, readers are left with a mystery surrounding the initials R. A. B., which are signed at the bottom of a note telling the

Dark Lord (Voldemort) that one of his Horcruxes (keepers for parts of a wizard's soul) has been taken away and replaced with a fake. Hermione, in her usual hardworking way, does heavy library research and discovers a couple of "reasonably well-known wizards" with the names of Rosalind Antigone Bungs and Rupert "Axebanger" Brookstanton, but "they don't seem to fit at all" because the person who stole the Horcrux appears to have known Voldemort and Hermione could find no association between these two wizards and Voldemort (636).

Phonological Fun

Rowling loves to play with the sounds of words, as shown by how much she enjoys alliteration, which is a well-recognized aid to memory. In her best examples, the alliterated sounds also hint at the meaning, as with Polyjuice Potion, and the name for a tailoring shop, Twilfitt and Tattings. The alliterative *m*'s in Moaning Myrtle's name sound like her constant "moaning." She is a ghost who lives in the bathroom plumbing, and when students flush the toilets they worry that she will rise out of the pipes for one of her doleful visits.

In a more somber example, the *s*'s at the beginning of Severus Snape's name might remind readers of the hissing of a snake when combined with the fact that his last name is only one letter off from *snake* and that he is the "severe" headmaster of Slytherin House. This fits with Rowling's desire throughout the books to make readers question whether he is "on the good side" or is really helping Lord Voldemort.

In her more playful moods, Rowling gives alliterative names to the passwords that Hogwarts students must give to enter various parts of the school. Toward the end of Book Four, Harry needs desperately to see Professor Dumbledore but he cannot remember the password. He frantically starts guessing with such phrases as Fizzing Whizbee, Drooble's Best Blowing Gum, and finally Cockroach Cluster, which, to his surprise, works.

Rowling also gives alliterative names to the students' books. *Spellman's Syllabary* is a fairly uninspired example when compared to such titles as *The Adventures of Martin Miggs: The Mad Muggle*, *Break with a Banshee*, *Gadding with Ghouls*, *Holiday with Hags*, *Travels with Trolls*, and *Wanderings with Werewolves*. Professor Lockhart distributes the longest list of required textbooks, topped off by his own autobiography, *Magical Me*.

Saucy Tricks for Tricky Sorts has the extra appeal of a reversal, while Rowling's name for Dr. Filibuster's Fabulous Wet-Start No-Heat Fireworks Shop is made more interesting by an ironic contradiction, which is also seen in the name of St. Brutus's Secure Center for Incurably Criminal Boys, which is where the Dursleys claim Harry spends the school year. Their own son, Dudley, goes to the Smeltings School, which might remind some readers of a school of fish. Another example of ironic alliteration is the Whomping Willow tree, which in character is as different as are the connotations of *whomping* versus *weeping*.

An amusing example of alliterative names with different connotations are the two names of Hagrid's hippogriff, which is a flying creature that is part horse and part griffin. His real name is Buckbeak, an appropriate reminder of a "bucking" horse and the "beak" of a large, vicious birdlike creature. But in Book Six, Dumbledore tells Harry that they have rechristened Buckbeak to Witherwings in hopes of keeping him from being recognized by the ministry, which had unjustly sentenced him to death. In the same book, a rumor gets started that Harry has a tattoo of a hippogriff on his chest, but Ginny Weasley puts a stop to it by announcing that it is really a Hungarian horntail.

When the Weasley family, along with Harry and Hermione, visit Fred and George Weasleys' Wizard Wheezes joke shop, they find that in the food section the brothers are offering Nosebleed Nougat and Puking Pastilles in their Skiving Snackboxes, along with their Ton-Tongue Toffee. The brothers offer three varieties of writing quills: Self-Inking, Spell-Checking, and Smart-Answer. They have also begun breeding cuddly little animals, miniature puffskeins, which they advertise as Pygmy Puffs, and they have brought in a few Muggle magic tricks, plus some Wonder-Witch beauty products for the girls. Their Fanged Frisbees are still selling well, while the Decoy Detonators are literally "walking off the shelves." Their new Extendable Ears enable Ron and Hermione to eavesdrop on Draco Malfoy when he is talking to the owner of Borgin and Burkes, a shop which sells "a wide variety of sinister objects" (124).

Playing with Morphemes

Morphemes are the smallest parts of language that carry meaning. By clipping morphemes from words and combining them with other morphemes,

Rowling creates all kinds of interesting names. The Kings Cross Station, where Harry is told to board the train for his first trip to Hogwarts, is a very real station in London, but of course it does not have a Track Nine and Three Quarters. The fact that, in preparation for going to Kings Cross Station, Hagrid had already taken Harry to Diagon Alley (a play on *diagonally*) has set readers up to expect that this is where he will "crossover" into a new world. And when he is cautioned against going into Knockturn Alley, where supplies for the dark arts are sold, readers grasp its forbidden nature because the name uses morphemes from such words as *knockdown*, *turndown*, and *nocturnally*, all words with more or less negative connotations.

Rita Skeeter is a reporter who writes malicious gossip for the *Witch Weekly*. She animages into a *beetle*, a word which repeats the long *e*'s of her name. But even before her ability to animage is shown, readers who refer to pesky mosquitoes as *skeeters* may have figured out that Rita Skeeter regularly "bugs" supposedly private conversations.

Omnioculars are an improvement over binoculars. *Omni* means "all" and whoever takes a set of Omnioculars to a Quidditch game can use them to put things in slow motion and to replay parts of the game. When the Weasleys go on a trip to Egypt, Ron brings Harry a Pocket Sneakoscope that emits a piercing whistle when it comes close to someone who is doing something untrustworthy or dishonest.

Even the word *Muggles*, which Rowling uses for people born without magical powers, is not entirely new. It was listed in the 1965 edition of *Webster's Unabridged Dictionary* as "origin unknown," but perhaps related to the word *mug*, which in Britain refers to someone stupid or easy to fool. American dictionaries define the verb *mug* as "calling attention to oneself by grimacing or making exaggerated gestures as for a camera," which in the view of most of the characters in the Harry Potter books is exactly what Muggles do.

Rowling was undoubtedly making an observation about the Muggle world when she created the word *mudblood* and treated it as an offensive term for someone who, like Hermione, have at least one parent who is a Muggle. Besides starting with the same sound as *Muggle*, it reminds readers of the words *half-blood* and *half-breed*, plus it has the negative connotations of *mud*.

In Book Six, another mysterious book plays a part in the story and, in fact, provides the title of *The Half-Blood Prince*. It is an old *Advanced*

Potion-Making textbook with notes written in the margins. Harry was given the book by the professor when he registered late for a class and his own book had not yet arrived from Flourish and Botts. The owner of the book, who refers to himself as *The Half-Blood Prince*, was exceptionally clever in noting improvements on the recipes and adding some totally original curses. To Hermione's irritation, the book gains Harry "a reputation for Potions brilliance" that he does not deserve (530). Hermione finally figures out through extensive library research that, in fact, the book belonged to Severus Snape, but she first suggests that the book might have belonged to a female student because she had found a picture "of a skinny girl of around fifteen. She was not pretty; she looked simultaneously cross and sullen, with heavy brows and a long, pallid face" (537). She was identified as "EILEEN PRINCE, CAPTAIN OF THE HOGWARTS GOBSTONES TEAM." Harry scoffs at the idea that the book's owner might have been female—he can just tell "it's a bloke," to which Hermione says, "The truth is that you don't think a girl would have been clever enough!" Harry responds, "How can I have hung round with you for five years and not think girls are clever?" (538).

When they go their separate ways, as angry with each other as they have ever been, Hermione goes back to the library and eventually finds a clipping about Eileen Prince marrying a Muggle with the last name of Snape. Later she finds another little news item about a baby being born to the couple, so indeed, Severus Snape was the owner of the textbook who had correctly identified himself as the "half-blood prince."

Sets of Names

Another way that Rowling aids the memory of her readers is to create sets of related names, both common and proper, so that a reader who remembers one of the names can probably remember the others in the set. For example, in creating the word *parseltongue*, for the language used between people and snakes, Rowling combined the image of a snake's tongue flicking in and out of its mouth with the grammar-related meaning of the verb *to parse*. Once readers understand the meaning of *parseltongue*, through analogy and context, they can figure out that a parselmouth is a person who speaks parseltongue.

A similar example is her creation of common names using the morpheme *mer* as seen in *mermaid*. The *merpeople* live under the sea and once she has led her readers to figure this out, then she can go on and refer to a *merperson*, a *mersong*, something *mermish*, and a *merversion* of a town square.

Many of Rowling's sets of words come right out of Halloween celebrations. The names of the four schools (Gryffindor, Ravenclaw, Slytherin, and Hufflepuff) have Gothic connotations connected to scary animals, even though the last one is just to the big, bad wolf in the "Three Little Pigs" who threatens to "Huff and Puff and blow the house down." The inn where Harry stays in Book Two is named the Leaky Cauldron, while the bar/restaurant is called the Three Broomsticks.

One of the names that Rowling gives to the high-stakes tests that Hogwarts students take is N.E.W.T., which stands for Nastily Exhausting Wizarding Tests. Newts are salamanders, a species associated with witchcraft, as when in Shakespeare's *Macbeth* the three witches mix a brew in their cauldron consisting of a newt's eye, a frog's toe, and a lizard's leg. Another name for the tests which students take when they are fifteen is O.W.L.s, which stands for Ordinary Wizarding Levels. This name is easier to remember because owls play an important part in the books by providing the postal system. Harry, Ron, and Hermione took their O.W.L.s at the end of Book Five just before they left Hogwarts for the summer, and so fairly early in Book Six they are waiting anxiously at the Weasley's Burrow for their owls to bring news of their O.W.L.s.

Ron names his messenger owl Pig. When Harry points out that the owl looks nothing like a pig, Ron explains that it is really a shortened form of Pigwidgeon, a name chosen by Ginny. Really, it is a name chosen by J. K. Rowling to fit in with the name of Hogwarts and the nearby town of Hogsmeade, where students can go to drink various kinds of mead.

Three important characters in the book, including Harry's father, James Potter; Harry's godfather, Sirius Black; and another student, Peter Pettigrew, had learned to animage when they were students at Hogwarts. They did this to protect their friend, Remus Lupin, who is a werewolf and needed to be watched over any time there was a full moon. To help readers recognize them in both of their shapes, Rowling devised names that "match" their alternate forms. Harry's father animages into a beautiful stag with a full head of antlers and is named Prongs. Sirius Black animages into a great black dog and is named Padfoot, while Remus Lupin is called Moony because he involuntarily animages whenever there is a full moon.

The other student, Peter Pettigrew, turns into a rat named Wormtail. He works for the dark side and disguises himself as a pet rat for Ron so that he can spy on the Weasleys, as well as on Harry. Ron innocently, but also fittingly, names his pet Scabbers, which fits with Pettigrew's traitorous actions. In Book Six, when he is back in his human shape and working for Severus Snape at Spinner's End, he is still called Wormtail and referred to as "vermin." He is described as hunchbacked having "small, watery eyes, a pointed nose, [and] a squeaky voice" (23).

Rowling also creates sets of names to identify the origins of students and faculty members coming from other schools. Viktor Krum is a champion Quidditch player who comes with his headmaster, Professor Karkaroff, from the Durmstrang school, which has the extra fun of reminding adults about the *sturm und drang* ("storm and stress" in German) theory of adolescent psychology. Madame Olympe Maxime comes from the "French" school of Beauxbatons, which translates as "beautiful wands," and so does Fleur Delacour.

At least a couple of Rowling's exotic names sound more foreboding, as with Azkaban, the prison guarded by the Dementors, and Nagini, the snake whose milk feeds the unrestored Lord Voldemort. Well-read children might remember the cobras, Nag and Nagini, from Rudyard Kipling's *Rikki-Tikki-Tavi Stories*. More neutral characters with names from India are Hassan Mostafa, the chairwizard and head referee of the International Association of Quidditch, and Hogwarts student Parvati Patil, named after the Hindu goddess.

Reinforcements

A clever and amusing technique that Rowling uses after someone or something has been named is to return to the name at a later time and to use it in a different way, usually in a joke. Rowling is probably doing this more for humor than for aiding memory; nevertheless both purposes are filled. Some authors give entirely different nicknames to their characters, which confuses readers, especially if they are listening to a recorded version of a book and so cannot easily go back to check on who is who. Rowling, however, is careful to make her additional names connect to the original name so that they serve as reinforcement rather than as confusion.

An early example is the surname of the Weasley family, which at first attracts little notice because it is attached to such ordinary names as Ron, Ginny, George, Fred, Percy, Bill, Arthur, and Molly. But as readers get to know the family better and get "invited" into their home, along with Harry and Hermione, the Weasley name is reinforced by the fact that their house is named the Burrow. The name is appropriate not just because the family name sounds like that of a species of rodents, but also because of the topsy-turvy fashion in which the living quarters were enlarged as each new child (or children, in the case of the twins) came along.

Hardly anyone needs help in remembering Molly Weasley's name, because from the very beginning when she spotted a confused and lonely Harry Potter trying to get on the train to Hogwarts at Kings Cross Station, she has served as almost a foster mother to Harry and Hermione, while also being the mother of Ron, Ginny, Bill, the twins Fred and George, and Percy. Because readers know her so well, they are almost as embarrassed as Harry is when near the beginning of Book Six, Rowling uses her name to lighten the fear that surrounds Lord Voldemort's return. Everyone is to give a password before they are let through a door. Harry is at the Weasley's Burrow where Mrs. Weasley and Tonks have been waiting anxiously for the late arrival of Arthur Weasley, the father of the family. When they hear him coming, Mrs. Weasley rushes to the door and says, "Arthur, is that you?"

> "Yes," came Mr. Weasley's weary voice. "But I would say that even if I were a Death Eater, dear. Ask the question!"
> "Oh, honestly . . . "
> "Molly!"
> "All right, all right . . . What is your dearest ambition?"
> "To find how airplanes stay up." (86)

Mrs. Weasley nods happily and turns the doorknob, but on the other side Mr. Weasley is holding it tight, while explaining that he must first ask Molly her question, "What do you like me to call you when we're alone together?"

> Even by the dim light of the lantern Harry could tell that Mrs. Weasley had turned bright red: he himself felt suddenly warm around the ears and neck, and hastily gulped soup, clattering his spoon as loudly as he could against the bowl.

"Mollywobbles," whispered a mortified Mrs. Weasley into the crack at
the edge of the door.

"Correct," said Mr. Weasley. "Now you can let me in." (86)

The most important "new" character introduced in Book Six, *Harry
Potter and the Half-Blood Prince*, is Horace Slughorn, a former teacher at
Hogwarts who Professor Dumbledore wants to entice back. Harry thinks
he is going to teach the Dark Arts class, but actually he ends up teaching
the Potions class, while Professor Snape teaches the Dark Arts class. Professor Slughorn is vain and "proud" of being associated with "important"
people and so on his recruiting trip Professor Dumbledore takes Harry
with him to the village of Budleigh Babberton where Professor Slughorn
is "hiding out" during the year of trouble over Lord Voldemort. Even
though Harry is not impressed at the professor's name-dropping, as when
he tells about getting free tickets from Gwenog Jones, the captain of the
Holyhead Harpies, and "a hamper every birthday" from Ambrosius Flume
of Honedukes, Professor Slughorn's vanity cannot resist the chance to
"gather" Harry into his circle (71). As Dumbledore and Harry are leaving,
Professor Slughorn comes to his door and calls them back to say he has
changed his mind and will come out of retirement. At school, Professor
Slughorn continues his old custom of courting "important" people and so
invites the children of prominent families to Sunday evening parties in his
quarters. The gatherings are referred to as "the Slug Club."

Mundungus Fletcher has questionable business practices, and when
people are disgusted with him for having stolen the things that he is
now selling, they refer to him as Dung. A more amusing name change
occurs with Fleur Delacour, the beautiful girl from Beauxbaton, the
French school for wizards. When Bill Weasley falls in love with her,
Ginny, Ron, and Hermione are so turned off by their open displays of
affection that they begin calling her Phlegm.

Dudley Dursely, who is a few months older than Harry, is the cousin
who is mean to Harry during all of his years of growing up. Readers
have known all along that Dudley is a *dud*, which makes it all the funnier in Book Five when Dudley is a teenager and wants to be called Big
D, but his mother still calls him by such pet names as Diddykins and
Dinky Diddydums. In Book Six, she progresses to calling him Dudders.

Draco's mother, Narcissa, is a lot like the mythological Narcissus,
who was so self-centered and vain that he fell in and drowned while

looking at his own reflection in a pool. In Book Six, after Lucius Malfoy has been sent to prison, Narcissa is left to manage the family interests. When she comes at night to beg help from Severus Snape, she and Bellatrix Lestrange (her sister who has spent years in prison) sound much like any two sisters who are not quite comfortable with each other, but are still willing to go together on a shopping trip or an adventure. Readers get a new insight into this as Bella calls out, "Cissy, wait!" and then argues, "Cissy—Narcissa—listen to me—" (20).

Allusions to Latin and Greek Myths

By choosing the name of Narcissa, Rowling was relying on people's familiarity with Latin and Greek mythology. Authors know that alluding to names of well-known people or items is an efficient way to make allusions, but choosing which names to use is challenging. For example, several years ago, author Richard Peck told us that when he wanted to refer to a popular teen idol he chose River Phoenix because he was young enough and popular enough that Peck assumed he would be "current" for the next fifteen or twenty years. But shortly after Peck's book was published, Phoenix died of an overdose, thereby "dating" Peck's book. J. K. Rowling does not have this kind of problem with the names from Greek or Roman myths that she drops into her books because they are as contemporary today as they have been for the past few hundred years.

Minerva McGonagall, the wisest and strongest of the women faculty members, is named after the goddess of wisdom, while Sirius Black, Harry's godfather, is named after the brightest star (the Dog Star) in Canus Major. He is the one who animages into a big black dog, the kind that has a long history in folklore and legends. However, in this particular case the "star" idea is the most important because until his death, Sirius is the brightest "star" in Harry's life.

Remus Lupin, a friend to both Sirius and Harry, is rumored to have a brother named Romulus, which will remind some readers of the twins who were suckled by wolves and grew up to become the founders of Rome. The connection to wolves is another example of how Rowling reinforces the names she gives her characters because *Lupin* is Latin for "wolflike," and ever since Lupin was attacked by Fanrir Greyback, he has been a werewolf.

An obvious Greek allusion is the name of Percy's owl, named after Hermes, the Greek messenger god. David Colbert says that Hermione Granger's given name is also a form of Hermes, which fits especially well with Hermione's personality because Hermes was not just a messenger, but also the god of communication and eloquence. Shakespeare used the name in *A Winter's Tale* for a character who is turned into a statue, which is what happens to Hermione in Book Two when a basilisk attacks her.

Aurors are the highest level of wizards. Their name comes from the Latin word for "dawn" and is familiar to English speakers from the Aurora Borealis. Argus Filch is a combination guard and caretaker at Hogwarts, who often observes Harry and his friends and reports them for breaking the rules. His first name is the same as that of the mythological giant with a hundred eyes, while his last name is slang for "stealing." Aragog is a great ancient spider, dearly beloved by Hagrid but not by anyone else. His name is taken from the species name of *arachnid*, which comes from the name of Arachne, the unfortunate young woman who dared to challenge the goddess Athena to a weaving contest. Arachne and all her descendants were turned into spiders so that they could go on weaving for the rest of time.

Professor Sprout's first name is Pomona, from the goddess of fruit. Madame Olympe Maxime's ancestors apparently came from Mt. Olympus, home of the gods. Nymphadora Tonks is named after the nymphs, who were beautiful forest maidens in both the Latin and Greek stories. Biologists have given *nymph* an extra meaning in relation to insects that go through a partial metamorphosis. Nymphadora Tonks apparently has the power to change her appearance as long as she is not depressed. That in Book Six she recovers her ability to change shows her happiness at Lupin's decision that they can find a way to be together even though he is a werewolf.

Latin-Based Names for Spells or Charms

Just as she does with English words, Rowling reminds readers that they are in a fantasy world by making slight alterations in the way she spells Latin root words and clips and blends them with other morphemes. The first time that Rowling uses one of her spells or charms, she devises a situation that clarifies the meaning. The charm is usually spoken by different characters, which lets readers come to it from various directions. Such repetition also gives readers time to associate it in their minds with words they probably know. For example in Book Six when the Death Eaters set Hagrid's cottage on fire as they flee from Hogwarts, Hagrid runs in to save his dog, Fang, and when he comes out the injured Harry smells "burnt wood and dog hair" and puts out a hand to feel "Fang's reassuringly warm and alive body quivering beside him." He tells Hagrid, "We should put out your house . . . the charm's 'Aguamenti . . .'"

> "Knew it was summat like that," mumbled Hagrid, and he raised a smoldering pink, flowery umbrella and said, "*Aguamenti!*"
> A jet of water flew out of the umbrella tip. Harry raised his wand arm, which felt like lead, and murmured "*Aguamenti*" too: Together, he and Hagrid poured water on the house until the last flame was extinguished. (605–6)

The "Aguamenti!" charm begins with *agua*, the Spanish word for "water," which is obviously related to several English words based on the Latin form of *aqua*, as in the name of a water-related color (*aqua* or *aquamarine*), and in such words as *aquarium* (a tank filled with water for fish), *aquifer* (an underground layer of water), and *aqueduct* (a large ditch or pipe built for carrying water over long distances).

"Lumos!" which brings light is one of Rowling's most obvious charms. It is based on Latin *lumen* as seen in such English words as *luminous*, *luminaries*, and *illuminated*. "Impedimenta!" is also recognizable because it slows someone down or stops them as if they have been tripped. It comes from the word *pedis* meaning "foot" as seen in *peddler*, *pedicure*, *centipede*, *pedestal*, and *pedestrian*. "*Sonorus!*" from *sonare* increases the sound of a person's voice and is seen in such English words as *sound*, *resound*, *sonata*, *sonorous*, *sonic boom*, and *supersonic*.

Rather than telling the story behind each of Rowling's charms, we will present a sampling of them in a chart, which will more efficiently illustrate the process. For clarity, we are capitalizing the Latin root. In instances when Rowling has relied on two Latin roots almost equally, we will make two rows so as to illustrate both meanings.

The items in these charts, as well as the earlier examples, provide only a sampling of Rowling's skill in creating names. Readers can have fun looking for other examples, especially in the forthcoming *Harry Potter and the Deathly Hallows*.

Magic Spell or Charm	Latin Root	Related English Words or Phrases
EXPELLiarmus! is a shouted charm that causes someone's weapon to fly away.	Expello, expeller–to drive out to expel	To be expelled from school To propel something Propellers on small airplanes and helicopters A propellant for an explosive
FELIX FELICIS is a good luck potion. The name comes from two forms of the same Latin root.	Felix, felicis–fruitful fertile	Felicitous The name Felix Greetings and felicitations Felicity
HORcruxes are "sacred" objects in which Lord Voldemort has stored parts of his soul in hopes of giving himself a kind of immortality.	Horreum, horri–barn storehouse granary	To hoard (Note: Although this is an Old English word, not a Latin root, it may still help people remember the meaning as when Horace Slughorn hoards things.)
HorCRUXES	Crux–cross gallows	The crux of the problem Something crucial The crucifixion To crucify
InCARCERous! is a verbal charm which binds people with rope.	Carcer, Carceris–prison jail cell	Incarcerate Incarceration
LEVIcorpus is a nonverbal curse which lifts its "victims'" bodies and hangs them upside down in the air. The countercharm is "Liberacorpus."	Levis, levies–light, not heavy	To levitate To elevate Elevation An elevator A levee Unleavened bread
LeviCORPUS.	Corpus, corporis–body	Corpse Corporation Marine Corps Corpsman Corpulent Incorporated
OCCLUmency is a spell which skilled magicians use to keep others from reading their minds.	Excludo, excludere–to shut out to exclude	To exclude someone To occlude something Occlusion To close

Magic Spell or Charm	Latin Root	Related English Words or Phrases
occluMENCY	Mens, mentis–the mind understanding reason intellect judgment	Mental Demented Mentality Mentally ill
MORSmordre! is the command that makes the Dark Mark, a sign of death, appear.	Mors, mortis–death	Mortal Morbid Mortuary Mortified Mortality Murder
OpPUGNO! is an attack command. Hermione gives it to a flock of little birds that she has conjured when she is angry at Ron for making out with Lavender Brown.	Pugno, pugnare–to fight to combat to give battle	Pugilist Pugnacious
PORTkeys are objects that have been "programmed" to take whoever touches them to specified places.	Porta, portae–a gate	Airports Seaports Passports Imports Exports
RENervate! is a spoken charm given with the idea of restoring a person's health or energy.	Renovo, renovare–to renew, to renovate, to repair	Renovate Renovation Renew
SECTumsempra! is a curse that wounds or cuts someone.	Seco, secare, secui, sectum–to cut	A religious sect A sectional couch To intersect something An appendectomy
SectumSEMPRA! causes wounds that are not supposed to heal, although Snape made a countercharm when Harry used the curse against Draco Malfoy.	Semper–always	The Marine Corps Pledge of Semper Fidelis means "always faithful."

Bibliography

Alexie, Sherman. *The Lone Ranger and Tonto Fistfight in Heaven*. New York: Grove Press, 2005.

Anderson, M. T. *The Astonishing Life of Octavian Nothing: Traitor to the Nation Vol. I*. Cambridge, MA: Candlewick Press, 2006.

Angelou, Maya. *I Know Why the Caged Bird Sings*. New York: Random House, 1970.

Bauer, Joan. *Hope Was Here*. New York: Putnam, 2000.

Block, Francesca Lia. *Baby Be-Bop*. New York: HarperCollins, 1995.

————. *Beautiful Boys*. New York: HarperCollins, 2004.

————. *Cherokee Bat and the Goat Guys*. New York: HarperCollins, 1992.

————. *Dangerous Angels: The Weetzie Bat Books*. New York: HarperCollins, 1998.

————. *Girl Goddess #9: Nine Stories*. New York: HarperCollins, 1996.

————. *Goat Girls*. New York: HarperCollins, 2004.

————. *The Hanged Man*. New York: HarperCollins, 1994.

————. *I Was a Teenage Fairy*. New York: HarperCollins, 1998.

————. *Missing Angel Juan*. New York: HarperCollins, 1993.

————. *Necklace of Kisses*. New York: HarperCollins, 2005.

————. *Psyche in a Dress*. New York: HarperCollins, 2006.

————. *The Rose and the Beast: Fairy Tales*. New York: HarperCollins, 2001.

———. *Violet & Claire*. New York: HarperCollins, 2000.

———. *Weetzie Bat*. New York: HarperCollins, 1989.

———. *Witch Baby*. New York: HarperCollins, 1991.

Booth, Coe. *Tyrell*. New York: Scholastic Push, 2006.

Cameron, Ann. *Colibrí*. New York: Farrar, Straus and Giroux, 2003.

Card, Orson Scott. *Children of the Mind*. New York: Tor, 1997.

———. *Ender's Game*. New York: Tor, 1985.

———. *Ender's Shadow*. New York: Tor, 1999.

Cisneros, Sandra. *House on Mango Street*. Houston: Arte Publico Press, 1983.

Cofer, Judith Ortiz. *Call Me Maria*. New York: Scholastic, 2006.

———. *The Meaning of Consuelo: A Novel*. New York: Farrar, Straus and Giroux, 2003.

Colbert, David. *The Magical Worlds of Harry Potter: A Treasury of Myths, Legends, and Fascinating Facts*. New York: Berkley Books, 2004.

Cormier, Robert. *After the First Death*. New York: Pantheon, 1979.

———. *Beyond the Chocolate War*. New York: Knopf, 1985.

———. *The Bumblebee Flies Anyway*. New York: Pantheon, 1983.

———. *The Chocolate War*. New York: Pantheon, 1974.

———. *Eight Plus One: Stories*. New York: Pantheon, 1980.

———. *Fade*. New York: Delacorte Press, 1988.

———. *Frenchtown Summer*. New York: Delacorte Press, 1999.

———. *Heroes: A Novel*. New York: Delacorte Press, 1998.

———. *I Am the Cheese*. New York: Pantheon, 1977.

———. *In the Middle of the Night*. New York: Delacorte Press, 1995.

———. *Other Bells for Us to Ring*. New York: Delacorte Press, 1990.

———. *The Rag and Bone Shop*. New York: Delacorte Press, 2001.

———. *Tenderness: A Novel*. New York: Delacorte Press, 1997.

———. *Tune for Bears to Dance To*. New York: Delacorte Press, 1992.

———. *We All Fall Down*. New York: Delacorte Press, 1991.

Curtis, Christopher Paul. *Bud, Not Buddy*. New York: Random House, 1999.

Cushman, Karen. *The Ballad of Lucy Whipple*. New York: Clarion, 1996.

———. *Catherine, Called Birdy*. New York: Clarion, 1994.

———. *The Midwife's Apprentice*. New York: Clarion, 1995.

Dunkling, Leslie. *The Guinness Book of Names, Sixth Edition*. Guinness Publishing, 1993.

Farmer, Nancy. *A Girl Named Disaster*. New York: Orchard Books, 1996.

Fitzgerald, F. Scott. *The Great Gatsby*. New York: Scribner, 1953.

Green, John. *Looking for Alaska*. New York: Dutton, 2005.

Green, Tamara M. *The Greek and Latin Roots of English, 2nd Edition*. New York: Ardsley House Publishers, 1994.

Hook, J. N. *Family Names: How Our Surnames Came to America*. New York: Macmillan, 1982.

Horvath, Polly. *The Canning Season*. New York: Farrar, Straus and Giroux, 2003.

Kadohata, Cynthia. *Weedflower*. New York: Atheneum, 2006.

Kerr, M. E. *Deliver Us from Evie*. New York: HarperCollins, 1994.

——. *Dinky Hocker Shoots Smack!* New York: HarperCollins, 1972.

——. *Fell*. New York: HarperCollins, 1987.

——. *Fell Back*. New York: HarperCollins, 1989.

——. *Fell Down*. New York: HarperCollins, 1991.

——. *Gentlehands*. New York: HarperCollins, 1978.

——. *Him She Loves?* New York: HarperCollins, 1984.

——. *I Stay Near You*. New York: HarperCollins, 1985.

——. *If I Love You, Am I Trapped Forever?* New York: HarperCollins, 1973.

——. *I'll Love You When You're More Like Me*. New York: HarperCollins, 1977.

——. *Is That You, Miss Blue?* New York: HarperCollins, 1975.

——. *Linger*. New York: HarperCollins, 1993.

——. *Little Little*. New York: HarperCollins, 1981.

——. *Love Is a Missing Person*. New York: HarperCollins, 1981.

——. *ME ME ME ME ME: Not a Novel*. New York: HarperCollins, 1983.

——. *Night Kites*. New York: HarperCollins, 1986.

——. *What I Really Think of You*. New York: HarperCollins, 1982.

Kliss, Kate. *Deliver Us from Normal*. New York: Scholastic, 2005.

——. *Far from Normal*. New York: Scholastic, 2006.

Krishnaswami, Uma. *Naming Maya*. New York: Farrar, Straus and Giroux, 2004.

Le Guin, Ursula K. *The Farthest Shore*. New York: Atheneum, 1972.

——. *Tehanu: The Last Book of Earthsea*. New York: Atheneum, 1990.

——. *The Tombs of Atuan*. New York: Atheneum, 1970.

——. *A Wizard of Earthsea*. New York: Parnassus Press, 1968.

Levine, Gail Carson. *Ella Enchanted*. New York: HarperCollins, 1997.

Martel, Yann. *Life of Pi*. New York: Harcourt, 2001.

Meehl, Brian. *Out of Patience*. New York: Delacorte, 2006.

Mosher, Richard. *Zazoo*. New York: Houghton Mifflin, 2001.

Myers, Walter Dean. *Monster*. New York: HarperCollins, 1999.

Napoli, Donna Jo. *Zel*. New York: Dutton, 1996.

O'Dell, Scott. *My Name Is Not Angelica*. New York: Houghton Mifflin, 1990.

Park, Linda Sue. *A Single Shard*. New York: Clarion, 2001.

——. *When My Name Was Keoko: A Novel of Korea in World War II*. New York: Clarion, 2002.

Paterson, Katherine. *Jip: His Story*. New York: Lodestar, 1996.

Paulsen, Gary. *How Angel Peterson Got His Name: And Other Outrageous Tales about Extreme Sports*. New York: Wendy Lamb Books, 2003.

Rapp, Adam. *The Buffalo Tree*. New York: Front Street, 1997.

Rosoff, Meg. *How I Live Now: A Novel*. New York: Random House, 1994.

———. *Just in Case*. New York: Random House, 2006.

Rowling, J. K. Book One: *Harry Potter and the Sorcerer's Stone*. New York: Scholastic, 1998.

———. Book Two: *Harry Potter and the Chamber of Secrets*. New York: Scholastic, 1999.

———. Book Three: *Harry Potter and the Prisoner of Azkaban*. New York: Scholastic, 1999.

———. Book Four: *Harry Potter and the Goblet of Fire*. New York: Scholastic, 2000.

———. Book Five: *Harry Potter and the Order of the Phoenix*. New York: Scholastic, 2003.

———. Book Six: *Harry Potter and the Half-Blood Prince*. New York: Scholastic, 2005.

———. Book Seven: *Harry Potter and the Deathly Hallows*. New York: Scholastic, 2007.

Ryan, Pam Muñoz. *Esperanza Rising*. New York: Scholastic, 2000

Sachar, Louis. *Holes*. New York: Farrar, Straus and Giroux, 1998.

———. *Small Steps*. New York: Delacorte, 2006.

Schmidt, Gary D. *Lizzie Bright and the Buckminster Boy*. New York: Clarion, 2004.

Simpson, D. P., Editor. *Cassell's Latin-English, English-Latin Dictionary*, 5th edition. New York: Macmillan, 1968.

Snicket, Lemony. *The Austere Academy: Book the Fifth*. New York: HarperCollins, 2000.

———. *The Bad Beginning: Book the First*. New York: HarperCollins, 1999.

———. *The Carnivorous Carnival: Book the Ninth*. New York: HarperCollins, 2002.

———. *The End: Book the Thirteenth*. New York: HarperCollins, 2006.

———. *The Ersatz Elevator: Book the Sixth*. New York: HarperCollins, 2000.

———. *The Grim Grotto: Book the Eleventh*. New York: HarperCollins, 2004.

———. *The Hostile Hospital: Book the Eighth*. New York: HarperCollins, 2001.

———. *The Miserable Mill: Book the Fourth*. New York: HarperCollins, 2000.

———. *The Penultimate Peril: Book the Twelfth*. New York: HarperCollins, 2005.

———. *The Reptile Room: Book the Second*. New York: HarperCollins, 1999.

———. *The Slippery Slope: Book the Tenth*. New York: HarperCollins, 2003.

———. *The Vile Village: Book the Seventh*. New York: HarperCollins, 2001.

———. *The Wide Window: Book the Third*. New York: HarperCollins, 2000.

Soto, Gary. *Accidental Love*. New York: Harcourt, 2006.

——. *The Afterlife*. Harcourt, 2003.

——. *Baseball in April and Other Stories*. New York: Harcourt, 1990.

——. *Buried Onions*. New York: Harcourt, 1997.

——. *A Fire in My Hands: A Book of Poems*. New York: Harcourt, 1990.

——. *Local News*. New York: Harcourt, 1993.

——. *Neighborhood Odes*. New York: Harcourt, 1992.

Spencer, Priscilla. What's in a Name? Your resource for Harry Potter name etymology. http://www.theninemuses.net/hp/. Accessed September 3, 2006.

Spinelli, Jerry. *Maniac McGee*. Boston: Little Brown, 1990.

Staples, Suzanne Fisher. *Haveli*. New York: Knopf, 1993.

——. *Shabanu: Daughter of the Wind*. New York: Knopf, 1989.

Tan, Amy. *The Joy Luck Club*. New York: Random House, 1989.

Voigt, Cynthia. *When She Hollers*. New York: Scholastic, 1994.

Yamanaka, Lois-Ann. *Name Me Nobody*. New York: Hyperion, 1999.

Index

After the First Death, 24, 31–33
Alexie, Sherman, xv, 103, 114–17
alliteration, 3–4, 128–29, 148
allusion, 4–5, 27–30, 34, 35, 156–57
allusions, smart, 125–28
Anderson, M. T., 117
Angelou, Maya, xv, 103, 108–10
animal names, 37–38, 44, 86–87
Arter, Lisa, 138
The Astonishing Life of Octavian Nothing: Traitor to the Nation, Vol 1: The Pox Party, 117–18
The Austere Academy: Book the Fifth, 125, 126, 130

Baby Be-Bop, 36–37, 44–45
The Bad Beginning: Book the First, 124
The Ballad of Lucy Whipple, 47, 57–62
Baseball in April and Other Stories, 66
Bauer, Joan, xii

Beatrice, 137–39
Beautiful Boys, 37
Block, Francesca Lia, xv, 23–24, 36–45
Booth, Coe, 122
Bud, Not Buddy, xii
The Buffalo Tree, 67–71
Buried Onions, 66–67

Call Me Maria, xv
Cameron, Ann, 119
The Canning Season, 18–22
Card, Orson Scott, xv, 83, 89–98
Carroll, Lewis, x
Catherine Called Birdy, 47, 50–56
celebrity names, xi–xiii, xiv, 38
Cherokee Bat and the Goat Guys, 36–37, 42–43
Children of the Mind, 89
The Chocolate War, 23, 24, 29–31
Cisneros, Sandra, xv, 103, 106–8
Cofer, Judith Ortiz, xv, 120

Colbert, David, 145, 157
Colibrí, 118–19
commercial names, xi, 8–9, 38, 67, 69, 85–86, 113
common nouns, 67–70, 82, 113, 129
Cormier, Robert, xv, 23–36
crossover (dual audience) books, 123–39
Curtis, Christopher Paul, xii
Cushman, Karen, 47–64

Dale, Jim, 141
Dangerous Angels: The Weetzie Bat Books, 37
Deliver Us from Evie, 7–8
Deliver Us from Normal, xiii
descriptive names, 48–49, 52–53, 143–46
Dilbert cartoons, xii
Dinky Hocker Shoots Smack, 1, 5, 6
doppelgangers, 131–34
doubles, 131, 134–37
dual audience (crossover) books, 123–39
Dunkling, Leslie, x

Earthsea books, 98–99
Ella Enchanted, xiv
The End: Book the Thirteenth, 124, 138–39
Ender's Game, 89–98
Ender's Shadow, 89
The Ersatz Elevator: Book the Sixth, 124, 127, 129
Esperanza Rising, 119
ethnic identification, xiv–xv, 41–43, 48–49, 96, 103–22

Family Names: How Our Surnames Came to America, 47

Far from Normal, xiii
Farmer, Nancy, 65, 75–82
The Fartherest Shore, 99
Fell books, 4, 9
A Fire in My Hands: A Book of Poems, 66
Fitzgerald, F. Scott, x, 34
food names, 40, 75

Gentlehands, 2, 6, 7
A Girl Named Disaster, 75–82
Goat Girls, 37
The Great Gatsby, x
Green, John, xiii
The Grim Grotto: Book the Eleventh, 128
The Guinness Book of Names, Sixth Edition, x

Handler, Daniel. See Lemony Snicket
Harry Potter books, 141–60
Harry Potter and the Chamber of Secrets, Book Two, 141
Harry Potter and the Deathly Hallows, Book Seven, 141
Harry Potter and the Goblet of Fire, Book Four, 141
Harry Potter and the Half-Blood Prince, Book Six, 141
Harry Potter and the Order of the Phoenix, Book Five, 141
Harry Potter and the Prisoner of Azkaban, Book Three, 141
Harry Potter and the Sorcerer's Stone, Book One, 141
Helquist, Brett, 124
Hemingway, Ernest, ix
Heroes: A Novel, 33–36
Him She Loves?, 3

His Dark Materials, 142
historical creation of names, 47–64
Holes, 12–16
Hook, J. N., 47–48, 30–51
Hope Was Here, xii
Horvath, Polly, 1, 18–22
The Hostile Hospital: Book the Eighth,
    126, 129, 130, 134
hostility/superiority, 2–3
House on Mango Street, 106–8
How Angel Peterson Got His Name:
    And Other Outrageous Tales about
    Extreme Sports, 10–11
How I Live Now: A Novel, 71–75
humor, 1–22, 55, 61–62, 72, 116–17
humor as a counterbalance, 7–8
Humperdinck, Engelbert, xi

I Am the Cheese, 24–29
I Know Why the Caged Bird Sings,
    108–10
If I Love You, Am I Trapped Forever?,
    2, 4
I'll Love You When You're More Like
    Me, 5, 8–9
illustrations, 124–25
imagined settings, 83–102
irony, 5–6, 13–16, 97, 124, 126
Is That You, Miss Blue?, 6–7

Jip: His Story, 119
The Joy Luck Club, 104–6
Just in Case, xiv

Kadohata, Cynthia, 103, 110–14
Kerr, M. E., 1–9
Kliss, Kate, xiii
Krishnaswami, Uma, 121

Latin-based names, 157–60
Le Guin, Ursula K., 83, 98–102, 142

Levine, Gail Carson, xiv
Lewis, C. S., 142
Life of Pi, 83–89
Linger, 6, 9
Little Little, 3, 7
Lizzie Bright and the Buckminster Boy,
    119–20
Local News, 66
The Lone Ranger and Tonto Fist Fight
    in Heaven, 114–17
Looking for Alaska, xiii
The Lord of the Rings, 142
Love Is a Missing Person, 2–3

magical realism, 37, 44–45
Maniac McGee, xii
Martel, Yann, xv, 83–89
ME ME ME ME ME, 2–3, 5
The Meaning of Consuelo: A Novel,
    120
Meehl, Brian, xiii
melodrama, 124–39
memorable names, 141–60
The Midwife's Apprentice, 47, 50–56
The Miserable Mill: Book the Fourth,
    124
Missing Angel Juan, xv, 36–37,
    43–44
mode, 23–45
Monster, 120
morphemes, playing with, 128,
    149–51
Mosher, Richard, 122
My Name Is Not Angelica, 120
Myers, Walter Dean, 120
mythological allusions, 156–57

name changing, 24–26, 34, 58, 85,
    99–101, 106, 107, 109–10,
    112–14, 115–16

name giving, 11, 30, 102, 105, 116, 118
name magic, 93
Name Me Nobody, 120–21
Naming Maya, 121
Napoli, Donna Jo, xiv
Narnia books, 142
National Book Award, 12, 18
Necklace of Kisses, 36–37
Neighborhood Odes, 66
Newbery Medal, 12, 47
Night Kites, 2, 5

occupational names, 48–49, 53–54, 58–59
O'Dell, Scott, 120
Out of Patience, xiii

palindrome, 13
Park, Linda Sue, xv, 122
patronyms, 54–57
Patterson, Katherine, 118
Paulsen, Gary, 1, 10–11
The Penultimate Peril: Book the Twelfth, 124, 130
phonological wordplay, 148–49
place names, xii–xiii, 18–19, 38, 48–49, 51–52, 57–58, 63–64, 65–57, 69, 72, 75–76, 88–89, 106–7, 128–29
plant names, 64, 75, 81
political terms, 94
Printz Award, 12, 71
psychological manipulation, 32–33
Pullman, Phillip, 142
puns, 4

Rapp, Adam, 65, 67–71
realistic settings, 65–82
reinforcing names, 63, 153–56

The Reptile Room: Book the Second, 124
Rosoff, Meg, xiv, 65, 71–75
Rowling, J. K., 141–60
Ryan, Pam Muñoz, 118

Sachar, Louis, 1, 12–18
Schmidt, Gary D., 118–19
Schwartz, Alvin, xii
A Series of Unfortunate Events, 123–39
sets of names, 151–53
Shabanu: Daughter of the Wind, 121
The Simpsons, 123
The Slippery Slope: Book the Tenth, 127, 133
Small Steps, 12, 17–18
Snicket, Lemony, 123–39
social class, 6–7
Soto, Gary, 65–67
spelling innovations, 146–48
Spencer, Priscilla, 147
Spinelli, Jerry, xii
Staples, Suzanne Fisher, 122
Star Wars movies, 142

Tan, Amy, xv, 103–6
Tehanu: The Last Book of Earthsea, 98–102
Tolkien, J. R. R., 142
The Tombs of Atuan, 99
tone, 23–45
totem names, 79–81
trends in naming, xiii–xiv
Tyrell, 121

urban legends, 83

Valdez, Jeff, 104
The Vile Village: Book the Seventh, 127
Voigt, Cynthia, xii

Weedflower, 110–14
Weetzie Bat, 23, 36–40
What I Really Think of You, 9
When My Name Was Keoko: A Novel of Korea in World War II, xv, 121–22
When She Hollers, xii
The Wide Window: Book the Third, 128, 130

Winter, Anne, xi
Witch Baby, 36–37, 40–41
A Wizard of Earthsea, 99, 142
word play, 3–4, 17–18, 20, 127–30, 142–60

Yamanaka, Lois-Ann, 119

Zazoo, 122
Zel, xiv

~

About the Authors

Alleen Pace Nilsen and **Don L. F. Nilsen** are professors of English at Arizona State University, where Alleen specializes in English education and Don specializes in linguistics. They are longtime members of the American Name Society and copresidents of the organization through 2008. Some of the chapters in this book developed from papers they presented at annual meetings of this group. Other books that they have written together based on their complementary interests include the *Encyclopedia of 20th-Century American Humor*, *Language Play*, *Vocabulary Plus: A Source-Based Approach K–8*, and *High School and Up*. Alleen is a founding member of ALAN, the Assembly on Literature for Adolescents of the National Council of Teachers of English, and coauthor of *Literature for Today's Young Adults* (with Ken Donelson), soon to come out in its eighth edition.